HOW
TO
PRACTICE

How to Practice

The Way to a Meaningful Life

His Holiness the
Dalai Lama

Translated and Edited by
Jeffrey Hopkins, Ph.D.

ATRIA BOOKS

New York London Toronto Sydney

ATRIA BOOKS
1230 Avenue of the Americas
New York, NY 10020

ISBN-13: 978-0-7434-2708-1
ISBN-10:   0-7434-2708-4
ISBN-13: 978-0-7434-5336-3 (Pbk)
ISBN-10:   0-7434-5336-0 (Pbk)

First Atria Books trade paperback edition August 2003

10   9   8

ATRIA   B O O K S   is a trademark of Simon & Schuster, Inc.

Manufactured in the United States of America

For information regarding special discounts for bulk purchases,
please contact Simon & Schuster Special Sales at 1-800-456-6798 or
business@simonandschuster.com

Contents

Foreword

I first heard His Holiness the Dalai Lama teach in 1972. Just three days after my arrival in Dharamsala in northern India he started a sixteen-day lecture series for four to six hours each day on the stages of the path to enlightenment. I had begun studying Tibetan and practicing Tibetan Buddhism in 1962, and my teachers, particularly gifted in the intricacies of Tibetan commentaries, had prepared me for study with Tibetan refugee scholar-yogis in India. But, to be frank, I did not think that a governmentally appointed reincarnation—born in northeastern Tibet in 1935 and recognized through prophecies, visions, extraordinary occurrences, and tests as the Fourteenth Dalai Lama at the age of two—could possibly live up to the billing.

However, I was amazed.

He spoke on a wide range of topics concerning the path to enlightenment, capturing my mind and heart with concepts, large and small, that clarified issues long unresolved, expanded on others, and drew me into new areas of understanding.

In Tibetan the Dalai Lama speaks with such great speed and clarity that it was impossible for me to be distracted. Once, he became particularly inspired while describing the reflections for generating compassion. His voice rose in pitch to a level that he jokingly described as his "goat-voice," in which I heard the inspired absorption of a poet. During that series of lectures he presented the full range of practices leading to enlightenment, often juxtaposing topics that others leave in isolation—all this with the depth of a philosopher. The same dual voice of poet and philosopher is present here in this book, sometimes touching the heart with moving descriptions of the condition of life and the beauties of altruism, and at other times making careful distinctions about profound practices like meditation on emptiness, which serve as nourishment for years of contemplation.

At the age of five the Dalai Lama was brought to

Lhasa, the capital of Tibet, where he underwent the full curriculum of monastic training. Due to the Communist Chinese invasion of eastern Tibet in 1950, he suddenly had to take the reins of Tibetan government at age sixteen. Despite attempts to cooperate with the invaders, he was faced with imminent, personal danger and escaped to India in 1959. In exile, he has successfully re-established centers for the broad range of Tibetan culture. He has traveled extensively throughout most of the world, bringing a message—not just to Buddhists and other religious believers, but to everyone—about the importance of kindness to the very fabric of society. In recognition of his untiring efforts on behalf of Tibetans and all peoples, he was awarded the Nobel Peace Prize in 1989.

His Holiness has published many books, some for a general audience and others for those particularly interested in Buddhism. In this book he draws on a long tradition of spiritual practice in Tibet and on his own experience to offer suggestions on how to practice a spiritual path that will lead to mental clarity and emotional transformation. In this way, he shows how life can be made meaningful.

Throughout the thirty years that I have known him and during the ten that I served as his chief translator on lecture tours in the United States, Canada, Indonesia, Singapore, Malaysia, Australia, Great Britain, and Switzerland, I have witnessed his embodiment of these practices to the very core of his being. It is important for us to recognize that this insightful, compassionate, humorous, and marvelous person rose from Tibetan culture. We need to value that culture as one of the world's great wonders.

Jeffrey Hopkins, Ph.D.
Professor of Tibetan Studies,
University of Virginia

HOW
TO
PRACTICE

Introduction

The Need for Peace and Kindness

I travel to many places around the world, and whenever I speak to people, I do so with the feeling that I am a member of their own family. Although we may be meeting for the first time, I accept everyone as a friend. In truth, we already know one another, profoundly, as human beings who share the same basic goals: We all seek happiness and do not want suffering.

TWO WAYS TO HAPPINESS

There are two ways to create happiness. The first is external. By obtaining better shelter, better clothes, and better friends we can find a certain measure of happiness and satisfaction. The second is through mental development, which yields inner happiness. However, these two approaches are not equally viable. External happiness cannot last long without its counterpart. If something is lacking in your perspective—if something is missing in your heart—then despite the most luxurious surroundings, you cannot be happy. However, if you have peace of mind, you can find happiness even under the most difficult circumstances.

Material advancement alone sometimes solves one problem but creates another. For example, certain people may have acquired wealth, a good education, and high social standing, yet happiness eludes them. They take sleeping pills and drink too much alcohol. Something is missing, something still not satisfied, so these people take refuge in drugs or in a bottle. On the other hand, some people who have less money to worry about enjoy more peace. They sleep well at night. Despite being poor in a material sense, they are content and happy. This shows the impact of a good mental attitude. Material development alone will not fully resolve the problem of humanity's suffering.

In this book I offer you, the reader, valuable techniques from Tibetan traditions which, if implemented in daily practice, lead to mental peace. As you calm your mind and your heart, your agitation and worry will naturally subside, and you will enjoy more happiness. Your relationships with others will reflect these changes. And as a better human being, you will be a better citizen of your country, and ultimately a better citizen of the world.

KINDNESS

We are all born helpless. Without a parent's kindness we could not survive, much less prosper. When children grow up in constant fear, with no one to rely on, they suffer their whole lives. Because the minds of small children are very delicate, their need for kindness is particularly obvious.

Adult human beings need kindness too. If someone greets me with a nice smile, and expresses a genuinely friendly attitude, I appreciate it very much. Though I might not know that person or understand their language, they instantly gladden my heart. On the other hand, if kindness is lacking, even in someone from my own culture whom I have known for many years, I feel it. Kindness and love, a real sense of brotherhood and sisterhood, these are very precious. They make community possible and thus are crucial in society.

THE HUMAN POTENTIAL

Each of us has a valid sense of self, of "I." We also share fundamental goals: We want happiness and do not want suffering. Animals and insects also want happiness and do not want suffering, but they have no special ability to consider how to achieve deeper happiness or overcome suffering. As human beings, endowed with this power of thought, we have this potential, and we must use it.

On every level—as individuals, and as members of a family, a community, a nation, and a planet—the most mischievous troublemakers we face are anger and egoism. The kind of egoism I refer to here is not just a sense of I, but an exaggerated self-centeredness. No one claims to feel happy while being angry. As long as anger dominates our disposition, there is no possibility of lasting happiness. In order to achieve peace, tranquility, and real friendship, we must minimize anger and culti-vate kindness and a warm heart. This can be achieved through the practices I will describe in this book.

Developing a warm heart ourselves can also trans-form others. As we become nicer human beings, our neighbors, friends, parents, spouses, and children expe-rience less anger. They will become more warm-hearted, compassionate, and harmonious. The very atmosphere becomes happier, which promotes good health, perhaps even a longer life.

You may be rich, powerful, and well-educated, but without these healthy feelings of kindness and compas-sion there will be no peace within yourself, no peace within your family—even your children suffer. Kindness is essential to mental peace. As you will see in the pages ahead, the central method for achieving a happier life is to train your mind in a daily practice that weakens nega-tive attitudes and strengthens positive ones.

The big question is whether or not we can practice kindness and peace. Many of our problems stem from attitudes like putting ourselves first at all costs. I know from my own experience that it is possible to change these attitudes and improve the human mind. Though it is colorless, shapeless, and sometimes weak, the human mind can become stronger than steel. To train the mind, you must exercise the patience and determination it takes to shape that steel. If you practice improving your mind with a strong will and forbearance by trying, trying, trying, no matter how many difficulties you may encounter at the beginning, then you will succeed. With patience, and practice, and time, change will come.

Do not give up. If you are pessimistic from the beginning, you cannot possibly succeed. If you are hopeful and determined, you will always find some measure of success. Winning the gold medal does not matter. You will have tried your best.

INTERDEPENDENCE

Much of the world is now connected by a web of electronic communication and instant information. In the twenty-first century our global economy has made nations and their people heavily dependent upon one another. In ancient times, trade between nations was not necessary. Today, it is impossible to remain isolated, so if nations do not have mutual respect, problems are bound to arise. Although there are grave signs of trouble between poorer and richer nations, and between poorer and richer groups within nations, these economic rifts can be healed by a stronger sense of global interdependence and responsibility. The people of one nation must consider the people of other nations to be like brothers and sisters who deserve progress for their homelands.

Despite the best efforts of world leaders, crises keep erupting. Wars kill innocent people; the elderly and our children die continuously, endlessly. Many soldiers who are fighting are not there by their own initiative; real suffering is experienced by these innocent soldiers, which is very sad. The sale of weapons—thousands and thousands of types of arms and ammunition—by manufacturers in big countries fuels the violence, but more dangerous than guns or bombs are hatred, lack of compassion, and lack of respect for the rights of others. As long as hatred dwells in the human mind, real peace is impossible.

We must do everything we can to stop war, and to rid the world of nuclear weapons. When I visited Hiroshima, where the first atomic bomb was dropped, when I saw the actual spot and heard the stories of survivors, my heart was deeply moved. How many people died in a single moment! How many more were injured!

How much pain and desolation nuclear war creates! Yet look at how much money is spent on weapons of mass destruction. It is shocking, an immeasurable disgrace.

Advancements in science and technology have greatly benefited humankind, but not without a price. While we enjoy the development of jet airplanes, for example, which make it possible to easily travel the world, enormously destructive weapons have also been created. No matter how beautiful or remote their homelands, many people live in constant fear of a very real threat: thousands upon thousands of nuclear warheads poised for attack. But the button must be pushed by someone, and thus human intention is ultimately responsible.

The only way to achieve lasting peace is through mutual trust, respect, love, and kindness. The only way. Attempts by global powers to dominate one another through competition in armaments—whether nuclear, chemical, biological, or conventional—is counterproductive. How can a world full of hatred and anger achieve real peace? External peace is impossible without inner peace. It is noble to work at external solutions, but they cannot be successfully implemented so long as people have hatred and anger in their minds. This is where profound change has to begin. Individually we have to work to change the basic perspectives on which our feelings depend. We can only do so through training, by engaging in practice with the aim of gradually reorienting the way we perceive ourselves and others.

The desperate state of our world calls us to action. Each of us has a responsibility to try to help at the deeper level of our common humanity. Unfortunately, humanity is too often sacrificed in defense of ideology. This is absolutely wrong. Political systems should actually benefit human beings, but, like money, they can control us instead of work for us. If with a warm heart and patience we can consider the views of others, and exchange ideas in calm discussion, we will find points of agreement. It is our responsibility—out of love and compassion for humankind—to seek harmony among nations, ideologies, cultures, ethnic groups, and economic and political systems. When we truly recognize the oneness of all humankind, our motivation to find peace will grow stronger. In the deepest sense we are really sisters and brothers, so we must share one another's suffering. Mutual respect, trust, and concern for one another's welfare are our best hope for lasting world peace.

Of course, national leaders have a special responsibility in this area, but every individual must also take the initiative, regardless of religious belief. Just by being human, by seeking to gain happiness and avoid suffering, you are a citizen of this planet. We all are responsible for creating a better future.

To achieve a friendly attitude, a warm heart, respect for the rights of others, and concern for their welfare you must train the mind. In this book I will present a series of practices drawn from Tibetan traditions that will be helpful in accomplishing these aims. The essential objective of daily practice is to cultivate an attitude of compassion and calm—a state of mind particularly crucial in human society today for its power to yield true harmony among nations, races, and people from diverse religious, political, and economic systems.

CREATING HARMONY

The harmony and friendship that we need in our families, nations, and the world can be achieved only through compassion and kindness. By helping one another, with concern and respect, we can solve many problems easily. Harmony cannot thrive in a climate of mistrust, cheating, bullying and mean-spirited competition. Success through intimidation and violence is temporary at best; its trifling gains only create new problems. This is why just a couple of decades after the enormous human tragedy of the First World War, the Second World War was fought, and millions more people were killed. If we examine our long history of hatred and anger, we see the obvious need to find a better way. We can only solve our problems through truly peaceful means—not just peaceful words but a peaceful mind and heart. In this way we will have a better world.

Is this possible? Fighting, cheating, and bullying have trapped us in our present situation; now we need training in new practices to find a way out. It may seem impractical and idealistic, but we have no alternative to compassion, recognizing human value and the oneness of humanity: This is the only way to achieve lasting happiness.

I travel from country to country with this sense of oneness. I have trained my mind for decades, so when I meet people from different cultures there are no barriers. I am convinced that despite different cultures and different political and economic systems, we are all basically the same. The more people I meet the stronger my conviction becomes that the oneness of humanity, founded on understanding and respect, is a realistic and viable basis for our conduct. Wherever I go, this is what I speak about. I believe that the practice of compassion and love—a genuine sense of brotherhood and sisterhood—is the universal religion. It does not matter whether you are Buddhist or Christian, Moslem or Hindu, or whether you practice religion at all. What matters is your feeling of oneness with humankind.

Do you agree? Do you think this is nonsense? I am not a God King, as some call me. I am just a Buddhist monk. What I am saying comes from my own practice, which is limited. But I do try to implement these ideas in my daily life, especially when I face problems. Of course, I fail sometimes. Sometimes I get irritated. Occasionally I use a harsh word, but when I do, immediately I feel "Oh, this is wrong." I feel this because I have internalized the practices of compassion and wisdom that form the core of this book. These daily practices are very useful and very valuable in my own life. Therefore, knowing that you and I are of similar mind and heart, I share them with you.

❖

When I was only fifteen, the Chinese Communists invaded eastern Tibet, and within a year the Tibetan government decided that I should direct Tibet's affairs of state. It was a difficult period as we watched our freedoms being eroded, and in 1959 I was forced to escape from the capital under cover of night. In exile in India, we faced daily problems ranging from our need to adjust to the vastly different climate to our need to re-establish cultural institutions. My spiritual practice gave me an outlook that made it possible to keep searching for solutions without losing sight of the fact that we are all humans led astray by wrong ideas and united by common bonds, ready for improvement.

This has taught me that the perspectives of compassion, calm, and insight are essential to daily life and must be cultivated in daily practice. Trouble is bound to come, so cultivating the right attitude is crucial. Anger diminishes our power to distinguish right from wrong, and this ability is one of the highest human attributes. If it is lost, we are lost. Sometimes it is necessary to respond strongly, but this can be done without anger. Anger is not necessary. It has no value.

I call compassion the global staple. Human beings want happiness and do not want suffering. Mental peace is a basic need for all humankind. For politicians, engineers, scientists, homemakers, doctors, teachers, lawyers—for all people in every endeavor—a healthy, compassionate motivation is the foundation of spiritual growth.

OVERVIEW OF THE BOOK

In the following chapters I will describe specific Buddhist techniques for gaining mental peace and a greater capacity for compassion within the framework of working to overcome what Buddhists consider to be wrong notions about how beings and things exist. In Buddhist terms, this is the path to enlightenment. However, anyone can make use of particular steps toward self-improvement as they see fit.

I have arranged this book in six parts. It begins with The Basics, where the story of the Buddha serves as a guide to meaningful living; here I introduce the three aspects of spiritual practice—morality, concentrated meditation, and wisdom—which are the book's principal themes. In the second part, Practicing Morality, I describe two types of morality: reorienting physical and verbal deeds so as to cause no harm to others, and cultivating deeper concern for others. In the third part, Practicing Concentrated Meditation, I describe how to achieve mental focus and how to restore calm in stressful situations. This is followed by Practicing Wisdom, which addresses the difficult but fruitful topic of dependent-arising and emptiness. Here we go deeper into Buddhist thinking as we consider the difference between the mind and its ultimate nature. In this fourth part I hope to clear up any notion that Buddhism is somehow nihilistic or pessimistic by describing the compatibility between appearance and reality.

These discussions of morality, concentrated meditation, and wisdom flow into the fifth part, Tantra, which presents a special yoga practice combining these three. I also discuss here how desire can be used in the spiritual path by competent practitioners.

The concluding part, Steps Along the Way, presents an overview of the path of practice from its beginnings right through to enlightenment, a state wherein mind and body are fully developed in order to be of service to others.

From beginning to end, our focus is on developing a good heart and mind through a moral attitude and an understanding of reality, empowered by concentration. Think of morality, concentrated meditation, and wisdom as a blueprint for enlightenment, reminding us of the highest aim of practice—a transformation of attitude toward peacefulness, compassion, calm focus, and wisdom. Understanding the blueprint is itself part of the path, drawing us toward the destination. I hope that parts of it may be of use, but if not, that is all right, too!

I
THE BASICS

I

Three Ways to Practice

Buddha's Enlightenment as a Model

According to some Buddhist schools, Shakyamuni Buddha first became enlightened in India in the sixth century B.C., through practice of the path. Others, however, believe that Shakyamuni Buddha had achieved enlightenment long before and that in his sixth century B.C. incarnation the Buddha was merely demonstrating the path. In Tibet, we take the latter view, and followers learn from his example how to practice in order to achieve enlightenment themselves.

In either case, we need to notice that:

- ◆ Shakyamuni Buddha was born into a life of pleasure as a prince in an Indian royal family. At age twenty-nine, upon seeing the suffering of the world, he gave up his royal position, cut his own hair, left his family, and took on the *morality* of a monastic, adopting a system of ethical behavior.

◆ For the next six years he engaged in ascetic meditation for the sake of achieving *concentrated meditation.*

◆ Then, under the Bodhi tree in Bodh Gaya, he practiced special techniques for developing *wisdom,* and achieved enlightenment. He went on to teach for forty-five years, and at age eighty-one, he died.

In the Buddha's life story we see the three stages of practice: morality comes first, then concentrated meditation, and then wisdom. And we see that the path takes time.

GRADUAL CHANGE

Developing the mind depends upon a great many internal causes and conditions, much like a space station depends on the work of generations of scientists who have analyzed and tested even its smallest components. Neither a space station nor an enlightened mind can be realized in a day. Similarly, spiritual qualities must be constructed through a great variety of ways. However, unlike the space station, which is constructed by many people working together, the mind must be developed by you alone. There is no way for others to do the work and for you to reap the results. Reading someone else's blueprint of mental progress will not transfer its realizations to you. You have to develop them yourself.

Cultivating an attitude of compassion and developing wisdom are slow processes. As you gradually internalize techniques for developing morality, concentration of mind, and wisdom, untamed states of mind become less and less frequent. You will need to practice these techniques day by day, year by year. As you transform your mind, you will transform your surroundings. Others will see the benefits of your practice of tolerance and love, and will work at bringing these practices into their own lives.

THE THREE PRACTICES

Buddha's teachings are divided into three collections of scriptures:

- ◆ The discipline of morality
- ◆ The discourses on concentrated meditation

♦ The manifest knowledge that explains the training in wisdom

In each of these scriptures, the main practice is described as an extraordinary state that is created from the union of (1) "calm abiding" (concentrated meditation) and (2) "special insight" (wisdom). But in order to achieve such a union, first we must lay its foundation: morality.

ORDER OF PRACTICE

Morality, concentrated meditation, and wisdom—this is the essential order of practice. The reasons are as follows:

♦ In order for the wisdom of special insight to remove impediments to proper understanding, and to remove faulty mental states at their very roots, we need concentrated meditation, a state of complete single-mindedness in which all internal distractions have been removed. Otherwise the mind is too fractured. Without such one-pointed concentrated meditation, wisdom has no force, just as the flame of a candle in a breeze does not give off much illumination. Therefore, concentrated meditation must precede wisdom.

◆ Single-minded meditation involves removing subtle internal distractions such as the mind's being either too relaxed or too tight. To do so we must first stop external distractions through training in the morality of maintaining mindfulness and conscientiousness with regard to physical and verbal activities—being constantly aware of what you are doing with your body and your speech. Without overcoming these obvious distractions, it is impossible to overcome subtler internal distractions. Since it is through sustaining mindfulness that you achieve a calm abiding of the mind, the practice of morality must precede the practice of concentrated meditation.

In my own experience, taking the vows of a monk called for fewer external involvements and activities, which meant that I could focus more on spiritual studies. Vows to restrain counterproductive physical and verbal activities made me mindful of my behavior and drew me to inspect what was happening in my mind. This meant that even when I was not purposely practicing concentrated meditation, I had to control my mind from being scattered and thus was constantly drawn in the direction of one-pointed, internal meditation. The vow of morality has certainly acted as a foundation.

Looking at the three practices—morality, concentrated meditation, and wisdom—we see that each serves as the basis for the next. (This order of practice is clearly demonstrated in the Buddha's own life story.) Therefore, all spiritual progress depends on a foundation of proper morality.

II

PRACTICING
MORALITY

2

Identifying the Scope
of Suffering

❖

Overview of the Types of Morality

The main principle of Buddhist morality is to help others and, if that is not possible, at least to do no harm. This fundamental commitment to nonviolence, motivated by concern for others, is central to the three types of morality in Buddhism:

◆ The morality of individual liberation (which is the subject of this chapter) is mainly practiced by refraining from physical and verbal actions that cause harm. This practice is called "individual" because it provides a way for a person to prepare to move beyond the repeated round of birth, aging, sickness, and death, which Buddhists call cyclic existence (or samsara).

- ◆ The morality of concern for others—called the morality of Bodhisattvas (beings primarily concerned with helping others)—is mainly practiced by restraining the mind from falling into selfishness. For those practicing Bodhisattva morality, the essential point is to refrain from self-cherishing, but also to refrain from ill deeds of body and speech.

- ◆ The morality of Tantra centers around special techniques for imagining a fully developed state of body and mind effectively helping others. It provides a way to restrain and thus transcend our limited perception of our bodies and minds so that we may perceive ourselves shining with wisdom and compassion.

MORALITY OF INDIVIDUAL LIBERATION

Practicing the morality of individual liberation requires the self-awareness needed to refrain from physical and verbal actions that bring harm to others. This means abandoning what Buddhists call the ten nonvirtues. These are organized into three categories. The physical nonvirtues are killing, stealing, and sexual misconduct. The verbal nonvirtues are lying, divisive talk, harsh speech, and senseless chatter. The mental nonvirtues are covetousness, harmful intent, and wrong views.

Since motivation precedes and drives actions, controlling it is the best way to prevent impulsive and possibly abusive physical and verbal actions. When you suddenly want something and just reach out and take it without considering the consequences, your desire is expressing itself impulsively, without benefit of reflection. In daily practice you learn to continually examine your motivation.

When I was a boy, Ling Rinpochay, who was then my junior tutor, was always very stern; he never smiled, not even a little. This bothered me a lot. By wondering why he was so humorless, I examined more and more what I was doing in my own mind. This helped me develop self-awareness with regard to my motivation. By my early twenties when I had matured, Ling Rinpochay completely changed; he always had a big smile when we were together.

Effective practice of the morality of individual liberation depends upon sound, long-term motivation. For example, one should not become a monk or a nun to avoid having to work at a worldly job for food and clothing. Also, it is not sufficient merely to seek to avoid difficulty *in this lifetime.* To be motivated by such trifling purposes does not help to achieve freedom from cyclic existence—the ultimate reason to practice the morality of individual liberation.

This is confirmed by Buddha's life story. One day Shakyamuni slipped outside the palace wall to experience life for himself. For the first time he saw a sick person, an old person, and a corpse. Deeply troubled by the suffering of sickness, aging, and death, he came to the conclusion that worldly life is without substance. Later, inspired by several religious practitioners, Buddha became captivated by the possibility of a higher, more meaningful, spiritual life. At that point he escaped from the palace, leaving his ordinary life behind to pursue that vision.

What does this teach us? Like Buddha we need to begin by becoming concerned about the suffering of cyclic existence and by turning away from temporary distractions. Influenced by this new attitude, we must take up a system of morality by renouncing cyclic existence and by taking vows of pure behavior through seeking to avoid the ten nonvirtues.

THE FOUR NOBLE TRUTHS

In order to free ourselves from cyclic existence we need to understand its nature. We need to (1) know the specific types of suffering involved, (2) discover the causes of those sufferings, (3) see if it is possible to remove those causes, and then (4) determine what should be practiced. Renunciation, therefore, involves at least a partial understanding of the four noble truths:

1. true suffering
2. true sources of suffering
3. true cessations of suffering and its sources
4. true paths for actualizing true cessations

When Buddha began teaching for the first time, he taught the four noble truths in the order just given. However, this order does not reflect how these truths come into being. In temporal sequence the second truth—the sources of suffering—precedes the first truth—suffering itself. Similarly, the fourth truth—the paths of practice—must precede attainment of the third—the cessations of suffering. However, Buddha taught the four truths in the order of *practice,* not in the order in which they are produced.

In practice, you have to identify the extent of suffering first, to know that this type of life is beset by misery; this deepens your natural wish to be freed from pain. When you recognize suffering for what it is, as Buddha did, then you will be drawn into discovering its causes, the sources of suffering. Just as a doctor must first diagnose a disease, you must understand the root cause of suffering before you can treat it. Not until you have determined the sources of suffering can you understand that there could be a cessation to it. Also, without decisively understanding that the end of suffering is possible, you might consider practice of this path just a fruitless hardship. Then you can seek the true paths for actualizing true cessations. This is why Buddha presented the four truths in the given order of practice.

I will discuss the first noble truth here and the next three in Chapter Three.

THE FIRST NOBLE TRUTH: SUFFERING

Suffering is like a disease we have all contracted. To find the cure we must carefully identify the full scope of the disease: pain, change, and pervasive conditioning.

1. One level of suffering is out-and-out pain that we all recognize as such. Even animals want to overcome it. The physical and mental pains of daily life, like headaches and the anguish of separation, fall into this category.

2. What we usually experience as pleasure is mostly a diminishment of pain. If good food or drink, for example, really were just pleasurable—if they had an inner nature of pleasure—then no matter how much we ate or drank, we would feel greater and greater happiness in equal measure. Instead, if we partake excessively, we begin to suffer in our bodies and our minds. This indicates that these experiences of pleasure have an inner nature of pain. I like to tell the story of a family that buys a new television. Compared to the old one, it is really great, and everyone watches it for days on end. But eventually they get tired of it. This indicates that the

original pleasure has a nature of pain. Such states of temporary happiness are called the suffering of change.

3. In addition to ordinary pain and the suffering of change, there is a deeper level of suffering called pervasive conditioning. Mind and body operate under the influence of karma (tendencies created by previous actions) and of afflictive, or counterproductive, emotions such as lust and hatred. In ordinary life we are born from and into the pervasive influence of karma and afflictive emotions. Even neutral states of feeling are under the influence of causes and conditions beyond your control—you are stuck in a process susceptible to suffering.

The Human Condition

At the beginning of our life is birth, during which we suffer, and at the end of our life is death, during which we also suffer. Between these two come aging and illness. No matter how wealthy you are or how physically fit you are, you have to suffer through these circumstances.

On top of this comes discontentment. You want

more and more and more. This, in a sense, is real poverty—always to be hungry, hungry, hungry with no time to be satisfied. Others might not be rich, but contentment provides them with fewer worries, fewer enemies, fewer problems, and very good sleep. On more than one occasion, when I have visited very nice homes in rich communities, I have peeked inside the medicine chest in the bathroom and found some medications to provide energy for the day and others to induce sleep at night. Contentment might do both of these jobs better since it reduces anxiety during the day, paving the way for sleeping peacefully.

In the frenzy of modern life we lose sight of the real value of humanity. People become the sum total of what they produce. Human beings act like machines whose function is to make money. This is absolutely wrong. The purpose of making money is the happiness of humankind, not the other way round. Humans are not for money, money is for humans. We need enough to live, so money is necessary, but we also need to realize that if there is too much attachment to wealth, it does not help at all. As the saints of India and Tibet tell us, the wealthier one becomes, the more suffering one endures.

Even friends can bring suffering. Usually we feel that friends bring us more pleasure and happiness, but sometimes they bring more trouble. Today your friend has a nice smiling face, but in a moment the conversation can turn sour, and you start to fight, with no trace of friendship. We do gain happiness and satisfaction from our friends, but it is impermanent; it is not true happiness. In a deep sense, ordinary friendship also has a nature of pain.

Look at your own body. No matter how smooth your complexion and how fine your figure, if you shed even one drop of blood, you are suddenly not so good looking. Under the skin there is raw flesh; look deeper and you find bone. Skeletons in a museum or a hospital make most of us uncomfortable, but we are all the same underneath. Some people may be quite fat, others thin, some handsome, yet if I look at them with an X-ray machine, I see a room full of skeletons with huge eye sockets. Such is the real nature of our body.

Consider the pleasure of eating. Today I had some delicious food. When I ate it, it was beautiful, but as it passed through my stomach and intestines, it changed into something not so beautiful. When eating, we avoid noticing that this is what happens, and we take pleasure, thinking, "Oh, now this is a very good meal! I am really pleased." But that beautiful food gradually passes through my body, and finally goes into the toilet in a form nobody regards as beautiful. This stuff that people regard as very dirty actually is made in this human body. In a way, making stool is a principal function of our bodies!

Eating, working, and making money are meaningless in themselves. However, even a small act of compassion grants meaning and purpose to our lives.

PERSISTENCE AND HOPE

Analyze. Think, think, think. When you do, you will recognize that our ordinary way of life is almost meaningless. Do not be discouraged. It would be very foolish to give up now. On those occasions when you feel most hopeless, you must make a powerful effort. We are so accustomed to faulty states of mind that it is difficult to change with just a little practice. Just a drop of something sweet cannot change a taste that is powerfully bitter. We must persist in the face of failure.

In difficult personal circumstances the best recourse

is to try to remain as honest and sincere as possible. Otherwise, by responding harshly or selfishly, you simply make matters worse. This is especially apparent in painful family situations. You should realize that difficult present circumstances are entirely due to your own past undisciplined actions, so when you experience a difficult period, do your best to avoid behavior that will add to your burden later on.

It is important to diminish undisciplined states of mind, but it is even more important to meet adversity with a positive attitude. Keep this in mind: By greeting trouble with optimism and hope, you are undermining worse troubles down the line. Beyond that, imagine that you are easing the burden of everyone suffering problems of that kind. This practice—imagining that by accepting your pain you are using up the negative karma of everyone destined to feel such pain—is very helpful. Sometimes when I am sick, I practice taking others' suffering to myself and giving them my potential for happiness; this provides a good deal of mental relief.

Every day in the early morning, and especially when I have the time, I do this practice in a general way with regard to all living beings. But in particular I single out Chinese leaders and those officials who must make decisions on the spot to torture or kill particular Tibetans. I visualize them, and draw their ignorance, prejudice, hatred, and pride into myself. I feel that, because of my own training, even if in reality I could absorb some portion of their negative attitudes, it could not influence my behavior and turn me into a negative person. Therefore, ingesting their negativities is not that much of a problem for me, but it lessens their problems. I do this with such strong feeling that if later in the day in my office I hear of their atrocities, although one part of my mind is a little irritated and angry, the main part is still under the influence of the morning practice; the intensity of the hatred is reduced to the point where it is groundless.

Whether this meditation really helps those officials or not, it gives me peace of mind. Then I can be more effective; the benefit is immense.

❖

Under no circumstances should you lose hope. Hopelessness is a real cause of failure. Remember, you can overcome any problem. Be calm, even when the external environment is confused or complicated; it will have little effect if your mind is at peace. On the other hand, if your mind gives way to anger, then even when the world is peaceful and comfortable, peace of mind will elude you.

❖

SUMMARY FOR DAILY PRACTICE

1. Examine your motivation as often as you can. Even before getting out of bed in the morning, establish a nonviolent, nonabusive outlook for your day. At night examine what you did during the day.

2. Notice how much suffering there is in your own life:

   ◆ There is physical and mental pain from sickness, aging, and death, which you naturally seek to avoid.

   ◆ There are temporary experiences, like eating good food, that seem to be pleasurable in and of themselves but, if indulged continuously, turn into pain: This is the suffering of change. When a situation switches from pleasure to pain, reflect on the fact that the deeper nature of the original pleasure reveals itself. Attachment to such superficial pleasures will only bring more pain.

- ◆ Reflect on how you are caught in a pervasive process of conditioning that, rather than being under your control, is under the influence of karma and afflictive emotions.

3. Gradually develop a deeper, more realistic view of the body by considering its constituents—skin, blood, flesh, bone, and so forth.

4. Analyze your life closely. If you do, you will eventually find it difficult to misuse your life by becoming an automaton or by seeking money as the path to happiness.

5. Adopt a positive attitude in the face of difficulty. Imagine that by undergoing a difficult situation with grace you are also preventing worse consequences from karmas that you would otherwise have to experience in the future. Take upon yourself the burden of everyone's suffering of that type.

6. Regularly evaluate the possible negative and positive effects of feelings such as lust, anger, jealousy, and hatred.

   ◆ When it becomes obvious that their effects are very harmful, continue your analysis. Gradually your conviction will strengthen. Repeated reflection on the disadvantages of anger, for example, will cause you to realize that anger is senseless.

   ◆ This decision will cause your anger to diminish gradually.

3

Discovering How Trouble Starts and Stops

❖

THE SECOND NOBLE TRUTH: SOURCES OF SUFFERING

After identifying the scope of suffering, we need to discover its sources, which are twofold: afflictive, or counterproductive, emotions, and contaminated karmas.

Afflictive Emotions

Since afflictive emotions contaminate karmas, or actions, I will discuss them first. There are two classes of afflictive emotions—one that is better expressed and the other that is better not expressed. An example of the former is a terrible fear from the past that becomes fixed in the mind. In this case, it is definitely beneficial to let your feelings out and discuss the incident.

When I was around fourteen years old during the summer at the Norbulingka Palace, the Regent (who at that time was my senior tutor) scolded me after a teaching that he gave annually. With a harsh demeanor, he said, "Even if your realization is equal to a god's, your behavior still has to conform to a human being's." I was hurt because I felt that I was already acting as an ordinary student listening to him even though I was the Dalai Lama, ranking above him. I was irritated and remained uncomfortable for the next few months. Then the Chinese Communists invaded eastern Tibet in 1950, and I had to escape from Lhasa to Tromo in southwestern Tibet near the Indian border. In time officials in Lhasa advised me that the situation looked workable and that I should return. While on the way back to Lhasa, we spent several days at the Regent's monastery, Talungdra. One day he asked during a casual chat whether because of his attitude I ever had become upset. I mentioned what had happened, somewhat vaguely, without much detail. What a relief this was! We went on to have a pleasant stay at the monastery.

It is better to talk about such things that occur only

once, whereas the other class of counterproductive emotions—which include such feelings as lust, hatred, enmity, jealousy, and belligerence—should not be expressed; they become more and more frequent. Expressing them tends to make them stronger and more prevalent. It is better to reflect on the disadvantages of engaging in such emotions and to try to displace them with feelings of satisfaction and love. We should forcefully overcome negative emotions when they appear, but it would be even better to find ways to prevent them in the first place.

Lust and hatred give rise to the other counterproductive emotions and thereby create a whole lot of trouble in this world. We cannot be content to live with the consequences of lust and hatred. Of the two, hatred is worse on an immediate basis because it so quickly brings harm to others, but lust is responsible for driving on the process of cyclic existence—the repeated round of birth, aging, sickness, and death—from lifetime to lifetime.

The root of lust and hatred is ignorance of the true nature of all living beings as well as ignorance of the nature of inanimate things. This ignorance is not just lack of knowledge but a consciousness that imagines the exact opposite of the truth; it misapprehends what is actually so. There are many levels of misperception, as in failing to understand what to adopt in practice and what to discard in daily behavior, but here we are talking about the ignorance at the root of all suffering. This is the notion that sentient beings and other phenomena exist inherently, in and of themselves. I will discuss this difficult topic later in Chapters Eight, Nine, and Ten.

Contaminated Karmas

All pleasure and pain depend on karmas, or former actions that have created predispositions in the mind. Karmas can be divided into virtuous and nonvirtuous according to whether they produce pleasure or pain in the long run. For instance, if the effect of an action is to establish a new human life, then that action is virtuous because its long-term effect is a good transmigration. Conversely, if the effect of an action is to cause your rebirth as a hungry ghost, then that action is nonvirtuous because its long-term effect is a bad transmigration.

Karmas can also be divided into those that etch the

general outline of a new lifetime by determining the type of birth as well as the length of life, and those that fill in the details of a lifetime, such as prosperity, good health, and so on. The former type is called a "path of action" because that action (virtuous or not) serves as a path, or a means, to a complete lifetime in either a happy transmigration or a bad transmigration. To be a "path of action," a karma must have four characteristics: motivating intention; correct identification of the person or object; proper preparation; and successful completion. Sometimes all of these factors occur, as in the case where you intend to give to a beggar and actually do so; sometimes only the motivation is present, and you intend to give to a beggar but do not actually do so; or you may get the result unintentionally, if some money drops through a hole in your pocket onto the sidewalk, and a beggar picks it up. Actions that do not have all four characteristics could fall into the second category, which fills in the details of a lifetime.

Finally, karmas can be divided into those performed by groups, such as organized charities, and those undertaken individually. The effects of karmas can be experienced in the same life, in the next life, or in a life after that. Strong virtuous or nonvirtuous karmas with a powerful motivation to help or harm can yield their effects during the same life.

The Process of Dying

In order to understand the types of karma and the special features of the highest levels of practice, we need to understand the dynamics of three stages: the process of death; the intermediate state between this life and the next; and the process of rebirth out of the intermediate state. The transmission of karmas from one lifetime to another occurs at death through a very subtle mind of clear light. Although this deepest level of mind exists throughout life, it is manifest at death, and therefore is often taught in this context.

You can learn more about this in many texts of Highest Yoga Tantra, spoken by Buddha, such as the *Guhyasamaja Tantra*. These texts describe the many different categories of mind or consciousness, ranging from gross to subtle. Subtler states of mind are more powerful and effective when applied in spiritual practice. The grossest level of consciousness perceives through the eyes, ears, nose, tongue, and body. More subtle is mental consciousness, which itself ranges from gross levels, such as ordinary thought, to deep sleep and fainting when the breath has stopped, to the innermost subtle mind of clear light. Except in extraordinary meditative states, the subtlest, or deepest consciousness manifests itself only when we are dying. (Less withdrawn and therefore brief versions of the subtle levels of consciousness also occur when going to sleep, ending a dream, sneezing, yawning, and during orgasm. I will discuss the last of these in Chapter Eleven.)

The process of dying involves a serial cessation, or dissolution, of the four internal elements: earth (the hard substances of the body); water (fluids); fire (heat); and wind (energy, movement). In ordinary life, these elements serve as the basis for consciousness, but during the process of dying their capacity to support consciousness decreases, beginning with the earth element. Each step in this dissolution actually increases the capacity of the next element to support consciousness. Step by step it looks like this:

1. When the earth element, or hard substances of your body, dissolves into the water element, the external indication is that your body becomes thinner; internally, you see what appears to be a mirage seen in a desert.

2. When the water element of your body dissolves into the fire element, the external signs are that the fluids in your body dry—your mouth dries, your nose puckers, and so forth; internally, you see what has been described as puffs of smoke from a chimney or smoke floating throughout a room.

3. When the fire element of your body dissolves into the wind, or air, element, the external indication is that the heat in your body diminishes; internally, you see what look like fireflies at night or like scattering sparks. Heat withdraws from the body in different ways—from the feet upward to the heart or from the top of the head down. The former is preferable because it indicates that the mind will exit the body either upward or straight forward, not downward, and thus will most likely lead to a favorable next lifetime. This is caused by virtuous karma.

4. Next, the wind, or movement of energy in your body, dissolves into consciousness, and your outer breath ceases; at this time you see an appearance like the light above a flickering candle flame when the fuel has almost been used up. (Some doctors would consider a person in this state to be dead, but from the Buddhist point of view the mere ces-

sation of the outer breath does not mean that consciousness has left the body.) The flickering light is
followed by the appearance of a steady flame.

The final four phases of dying involve the dissolution of grosser levels of consciousness into subtler. This
happens when the winds, or inner energies, that serve as
the mounts of consciousness dissolve. Think of consciousness as mounted on energy like a rider on a horse.
In preparation for the next phase, the energies that
served as the mounts of the many types of conceptual
consciousnesses dissolve, shifting the basis of consciousness from grosser to subtler levels of energy. These naturally occur in four phases:

5. Your mind itself turns into an omnipresent, huge,
   vivid white vastness. It is described as a clear sky
   filled with moonlight—not the moon shining in
   empty space but that space filled with white light.
   Conceptual thought has vanished, and nothing
   appears except this vivid whiteness, which is your
   consciousness. However, a subtle sense of subject
   and object remains, so the state is slightly dualistic.
6. Your mind turns into a red or orange vastness, more

vivid than before; nothing else appears. It is like a clear sky filled with sunlight—not the sun shining in the sky but space itself, filled with red or orange light. In this state the mind is even less dualistic.

7. Your mind itself turns into a still more subtle, vividly black state; nothing else appears. This is called "near-attainment" because you are close to manifesting the mind of clear light. The mind of black vastness is like a moonless, very dark sky just after dusk when no stars are seen. In the beginning of this phase you are aware, but then you lose awareness as you slip into even thicker darkness.

8. When the mind of black appearance ceases, your mind itself turns into the fully aware mind of clear light. Called the fundamental innate mind of clear light, this is the most subtle, profound, and powerful level of consciousness. It is like the sky's natural state at dawn (not sunrise)—without moonlight, sunlight, or darkness.

The passage through to the mind of clear light can be fast or slow. Some people remain in the final stage, the mind of clear light of death, for only several minutes; others stay for as long as a week or two. Since the mind of clear light is so powerful, it is valuable to practice, so many Tibetan practitioners rehearse these stages of dying on a daily basis. I myself practice them six times daily by imagining the eight levels of mind one by one (without, of course, the physical changes in the first four stages). The eight levels of mind are:

1. mirage
2. smoke
3. fireflies
4. flame of a candle
5. vivid white sky-mind
6. vivid red or orange sky-mind
7. vivid black sky-mind
8. clear light

In the process of dying, we know that the person is still in the clear light as long as the body does not begin to smell or rot. There are Tibetans who have been tortured and, upon being returned to their jail cells, sit cross-legged in the process of death, sustaining the mind of clear light. Reportedly, their Chinese Communist prison guards have been amazed by this. From the viewpoint of their own dogmatism, they regard Buddhism as blind faith, so when they are faced with such evidence, they try to keep quiet about it. In India, too, quite a number of practitioners have remained in this state, sometimes for a few days and in one case for around seventeen days. When a person is abiding in the state of clear light, if the energy that supports this deep level of mind begins to fluctuate, at that point consciousness finally leaves the body, and the body or head shifts slightly.

There are many opportunities for further investigation into the various stages of death. Modern science has done a great deal of research on energy waves, the human brain, and its functions. Scientists and Buddhists share a common interest in this area, and I believe we should work together to probe the relationship between the mind and its inner energies, and between the brain and consciousness. Buddhist explanations can contribute to scientific research, and vice versa. This kind of cooperation is already underway, and more would be helpful.

Intermediate State

All beings who are to be reborn as humans pass through an intermediate state between this lifetime and the next. In this intermediate state your body takes on a shape that resembles your body in the next life at age five or six (although some say this is not necessarily so). When the intermediate life ends, the bridge to the next lifetime has been crossed. This process is carried out by the subtlest level of mind.

The Process of Rebirth

With regard to rebirth, consciousness enters the womb when the male and female fertilizing elements mix together—provided there is nothing wrong in the womb or with the sperm, and provided all the favorable factors such as karmic connection are present. However, consciousness does not necessarily have to enter at the time when the male and female are in union, for in our texts there are accounts of the father's semen being inserted into the vagina separately from intercourse. It seems that whether these elements come together inside or, as sometimes is the case nowadays, outside the womb in vitro, consciousness would have to enter while they mix. Still, it is difficult to arrive at a decisive explanation from Buddhist texts since some books say that fertilization takes place when male and female are at a point of strong desire.

This complex subject becomes more complicated in modern times. Consider an instance when an embryo is refrigerated. Once the connection has been made from the past life to the new life through fertilization, would that being whose embryonic body is refrigerated undergo the suffering of cold? The very beginning of the body has already been established, and so, according to our explanations, the organ of bodily feeling has already primitively formed (even though the organs of vision and so forth have not). Is there physical sensation from the next moment after fertilization? I have not come to a decision on these points; they are topics for much discussion.

If we assume that the being in the embryo does suffer cold, this raises the question of whether the person who puts the embryo in the refrigerator accumulates bad karma from that action. This would depend on the person's motivation. We cannot say that just because another being undergoes suffering due to something that is somehow involved with you, you would accumulate bad karma. For instance, even in normal circumstances a fetus in the mother's womb undergoes suffering due to being in the womb, but the mother does not accumulate any bad karma. Similarly, when the child is born, it suffers again, but the mother does not accumulate any bad karma. (If she did, a mother who gave birth to many children would have accumulated a great deal of bad karma, which is absurd!) Therefore, a person's motivation is the key to determine what type of karma accumulates.

THE THIRD NOBLE TRUTH:
TRUE CESSATIONS

Since defilements of the mind such as lust, hatred, jealousy, and belligerence are based on a fundamental misconception of the nature of persons and objects, the process of overcoming them requires a solution to that ignorance. The question becomes how to uproot the ignorance that is the cause of suffering. It cannot be pulled out like a thorn or removed through surgery. In order to overcome this misconception of the nature of persons and things, you have to understand their true nature. Then, through continued meditation, you become accustomed to the truth and increase the power of wisdom to undermine negative emotions rooted in ignorance.

At this point an explanation of emptiness would be helpful since this is what wisdom realizes about the nature of persons and things (see Chapters Eight–Ten).

But, in brief, the fact that defilements such as afflictive emotions can be extinguished at all is due to the mind not being impure by nature. It has a pure essence. Defilements are purified through meditation on the true nature both of the mind and of all other things. Extinguishing these defilements is the third noble truth of cessation—a state beyond suffering and its causes.

THE FOURTH NOBLE TRUTH: TRUE PATHS

True paths refer to three ways of training that are the principal topics of this book—morality, concentrated meditation, and wisdom. Spiritual practice along these paths leads to true cessations, culminating in nirvana and eventually Buddhahood.

From beginningless time we have had a valid awareness, or consciousness, of "I." This "I," or self, naturally and innately wants happiness and does not want suffering, and this desire is valid—it is true and reasonable. Consequently, all of us have the right to achieve happiness and banish suffering. The fact that suffering and happiness themselves change from moment to moment indicates that these experiences depend upon causes and conditions. In order to get rid of suffering we need to eliminate the causes and conditions of suffering, and in order to achieve happiness we need to acquire the causes and conditions of happiness.

The first two noble truths apply to the impure phenomena which we want to get rid of—true sufferings, which are the effects, and true sources, which are the causes. The final two noble truths are pure states which we want to attain—true cessations, which are the effects, and true paths, which are the causes. The way Buddha taught the four noble truths they contain two sequences—one of suffering, which we seek to abandon, and one of happiness, which we seek to adopt.

❖

SUMMARY FOR DAILY PRACTICE

Having recognized the scope of suffering, research its causes, or sources, and identify that the source of suffering is ignorance of the true nature of persons and things, which results in lust, hatred, and so forth. Realize that suffering can be removed, it can be extinguished into the sphere of reality. Reflect that this true cessation is attained through the practice of morality, concentrated meditation, and wisdom—the true paths.

4

Refraining from Harm

❖

Buddhists take a vow of morality in the context of first taking refuge—in Buddha, in the states of realization, and in the spiritual community. Refuge is the foundation for the practice of morality. Buddha teaches us how to find refuge from suffering and limitation, but the chief refuge, or source of protection, is found in the states of realization achieved through practicing morality, concentrated meditation, and wisdom.

Buddhist scriptures recommend that you hide your good qualities and achievements like a lamp inside a vessel. You should not advertise them unless there is great purpose in doing so. It is considered a minor infraction of a monastic's vow if he or she achieves the state of liberation and says to someone else, "I have attained liberation." This being the case, it is difficult to determine what stage of inner experience another person has achieved. I have had the opportunity to meet several people who have attained extraordinary spiritual development. There was a not very scholarly monk from my Namgyel monastery who came out of Tibet to India around 1980. Since we knew each other, we were casually chatting one day. He told me that while he was in a Chinese Communist gulag for almost eighteen years, he faced danger on a few occasions. I thought he was referring to a threat to his own life. But when I asked, "What danger?" he answered, "Losing compassion toward the Chinese." He considered this to be the danger! Most of us would feel proud to tell others about how angry we got, as if we were some kind of hero.

A lama from the Drukpa Kagyu tradition and I were very close. We met frequently and always used to joke, teasing each other back and forth. On one occasion I asked him about his spiritual experience. He told me that when he was young, he was staying with his lama who had him perform the preliminary practice of making a hundred thousand prostrations to the Buddha, the doctrine, and the spiritual community. Early in the morning and late in the evening he had to make prostrations on a low platform the length of his body. His lama was meditating in the dark in the next room; so to trick him into thinking he was making prostrations he would tap with his knuckles on the prostration platform. Years later, after his lama passed away, he was taking a meditation retreat in a cave, during which he recalled his lama's great kindness over years of training him, and he wept and wept. He almost fainted, but then experienced the clear light, which he continuously practiced. Subsequently, after successful meditations he occasionally would remember past lives in vivid reflections before him.

These firsthand stories have inspired me. There are definitely practitioners today moving in the direction of Buddhahood. Meeting these people increases our inspiration and determination, and through them the teaching becomes alive. In this way the spiritual community provides models for practitioners to look up to, which can help lead us to refuge.

These three—the Buddha, the states of realization and doctrines that teach them, and the spiritual community—are factors outside yourself that have greater capacity to end suffering than you presently do. However, a Buddhist is not asking them to grant happiness. Rather, happiness comes from putting the doctrine into practice. Buddha teaches the actual refuge—how to practice the doctrine—but the main responsibility lies in your own implementation. To create the foundation for an eventual spiritual state devoid of suffering and limitation we need to engage in the following practice:

1. Identify the ten nonvirtues (see p. 29).
2. Identify the ten virtues (which are the opposites of those nonvirtues).
3. Abandon the former and adopt the latter.

LEVELS OF PRACTICE OF THE MORALITY OF INDIVIDUAL LIBERATION

Because people vary in their ability to keep certain vows, Buddha described several different levels of moral practice. Within the morality of individual liberation, there are:

♦ those who live a householder's life, in a home rather than a monastery
♦ those who have left a householder's life to become nuns or monks.

If you are capable of maintaining chastity for a lifetime, you can leave the household and take monastic vows. If you cannot maintain chastity but can keep vows, you can take certain layperson's vows that last an entire lifetime, or others that last for only a day.

BENEFITS OF MORALITY

We find many similarities in the monastic life in all religions—simplicity, devotion through prayer or meditation, and service to others. Christian clergy are especially committed to service in the fields of education, health, and welfare, and Buddhist monastics have much to learn from these Christian traditions.

Practice of the morality of individual liberation, whether lay or monastic, leads to contentment. For example, monastics adhere to a limited diet—a small breakfast and then lunch, with nothing after that. They have no right to demand, "I want this food or that." Whatever they are offered on daily rounds of begging, they must accept. Thus Buddhist monastics are not necessarily vegetarian; whatever they get, they will eat. That is the training of *contentment regarding food.* It alleviates anxiety about getting this or that kind of food. Lay people can emulate this practice by not insisting on special foods. Even if you are rich, you actually cannot consume much more than poor people, except to your own detriment. Both rich and poor have the same stomach.

With regard to clothing, monks and nuns are limited to only one set of robes. To own more than one, he or she must get the blessing of another monastic, keeping in mind that the extra robe also belongs to the other person. We cannot wear expensive clothing. Prior to the Communist Chinese invasion, monks and nuns sometimes wore luxurious clothes, which amounted to corruption and self-deception. (In a way, the Communist Chinese have been kind to us by destroying these corruptions!) This limitation in dress is the practice of *contentment regarding clothes.* Lay people can adopt a similar practice through moderation in dress. The same is true for adornments. Wearing more than one ring on each finger is certainly too much! It is a mistake to think that it is really worthwhile to spend more on food, clothing, and adornments just because you have more money. Rather, spend more on health and education for poor people. This is not forced socialism but voluntary compassion.

Also it is essential for monastics to be satisfied with adequate shelter. An elaborate home is not allowed. This is called *contentment with regard to shelter.* Lay people can adapt this practice by reducing the neverending quest for a better home and for the furniture and decorations in it.

Examine your attitudes toward food, clothes, and shelter. By reducing expectations you will promote contentment. The extra energy which is released should be devoted to meditation and to achieve cessation of problems, corresponding to the fourth and third noble truths. In this way, contentment is the basis, and the resulting action is called *liking meditation and abandonment.*

We should be contented in material areas, for those are bound by limitation, but not with regard to the spiritual, which can be extended limitlessly. Though it is true that a discontented person who owned the whole world might want to own a tourist center on the moon, that person's life is limited, and even the amount that can be owned is limited. It is better right from the beginning to be contented. However, with regard to compassion and altruism there is no limit, and thus we should not be content with the degree that we have. We are just the opposite; in the spiritual field we are content with slight amounts of practice and progress, but materially we always want more and more. It should be the other way around. Everyone needs to practice this, whether lay or monastic.

Practicing the morality of individual liberation is also helpful in increasing mindfulness and introspection. If a monastic is about to commit certain acts even in a dream, he or she realizes "I am a monk/nun; I should not act this way." Mindfulness comes from a highly developed awareness of your physical and verbal actions, which carries over into dream-time. If you pay close attention to your conduct when eating, coming and going, sitting and standing, and so forth, then a strong condition of mindfulness will take hold.

The practice of the morality of individual liberation also fosters tolerance and patience. Buddha said that patience is the highest form of asceticism, and through it one can reach nirvana. For monks and nuns, there are four qualities of patience and tolerance to maintain:

- If someone pushes you around, you should be tolerant, patient
- If someone shows anger to you, you should not respond with anger
- If someone hits you, you should not strike back

◆ If someone embarrasses and insults you, you should not answer back

These practices increase patience. A person who has left the householder's life but hurts someone else is not engaged in proper activity. There are stories of monks in Tibet who have even gone to war! They threw themselves into battle despite Buddha's repeated teaching that to harm anyone else is certainly not virtuous for a monk or nun.

Spiritual practice is not about externals—food, clothes, or the like. Spiritual practice takes place in our hearts, in our minds. "True change is within; leave the outside as it is." If your behavior truly reflects an improved mind and heart, that is fine. However, if you are just making a show of your spiritual accomplishments in order to get money, for example, that is hypocrisy.

Practicing Buddhism means transforming your attitude. Monastic practices can be incorporated into a layperson's life through a strong, conscious wish to refrain from harming others, physically or verbally. This requires patience that will withstand physical and verbal attack.

A gradual approach is far better than trying to jump too high too soon; otherwise, there is great risk and danger.

For the time being, contribute to society and practice the teachings. Once you reach a certain stage of experience, you can practice with greater force if you become a monastic. These practices fit together step by step.

Usually my advice for beginners is to be patient; have fewer expectations of yourself. It is most important to be an honest citizen, a good member of the human community. Whether or not you understand profound ideas, it is important to be a good person wherever you are right now. You should not neglect a greater purpose for the sake of a smaller one. Consider both the present and the long term, in the same way that temporary economic gains should be considered in relation to long-term environmental needs.

❖

I like to say that the essence of the Buddha's teaching can be found in two sayings:

If possible, you should help others.
If that is not possible, at least you should do no harm.

Refraining from harming others is the essence of the initial stage of living the teachings of morality.

SUMMARY FOR DAILY PRACTICE

1. Notice your attachments to food, clothes, and shelter, and adapt monastic practices of contentment to a layperson's life. Be satisfied with adequate food, clothing, and shelter. Use the additional free time for meditation so that you can overcome more problems.

2. Develop a strong desire to refrain from harming others either physically or verbally no matter whether you are embarrassed, insulted, reviled, pushed, or hit.

5

Extending Help

❖

With the practice of doing no harm as your foundation, now you can cultivate concern for others. First, through the morality of individual liberation, we learned to control anger and the like, and now we can begin learning how to comfort and serve others. The practices described in Chapters Two through Four— abandoning the ten nonvirtues, identifying the scope and process of suffering and the way beyond it through the four noble truths, and adapting the monastic's detachment from transient pleasures to a layperson's life—all create a necessary background for the second stage, what we call the morality of the Great Vehicle.

Now, not only do you not harm others, but you carry more responsibility for helping them. Not harming others is a defensive practice, whereas the move to help others is proactive.

Buddha teaches three stages of morality: the morality of individual liberation, the morality of concern for others, and the morality of Tantra. Helping others is the Great Vehicle teaching, the heart of the second stage, or Bodhisattva morality. It is also the focus of this chapter.

THE VALUE OF DIFFICULT CIRCUMSTANCES

How can you cultivate this other-concerned attitude? The main approach for orienting yourself toward caring is to consider your importance relative to others. A practice that traveled from India to Tibet involves first finding common ground with others (equalizing) and then replacing your self-centeredness with other-centeredness. The Indian scholar-yogi Shantideva explains this practice of equalizing and switching self and other thoroughly in his *A Guide to the Bodhisattva Way of Life,* and many Tibetans have written commentaries on his text.

Real compassion extends to each and every sentient being, not just to friends or family or those in terrible situations. To develop the practice of compassion to its fullest extent, one must practice patience. Shantideva tells us that if the practice of patience really moves your mind and brings about a change, you will begin to see your enemies as the best of friends, even as spiritual guides.

Enemies provide us some of the best opportunities to practice patience, tolerance, and compassion. Shantideva gives us many marvelous examples of this in the form of dialogues between positive and negative aspects of one's own mind. His reflections on compassion and patience have been very useful in my own practice. Read them and your whole soul can be transformed. Here is an example:

> For a practitioner of love and compassion, an enemy is one of the most important teachers. Without an enemy you cannot practice tolerance, and without tolerance you cannot build a sound basis of compassion. So in order to practice compassion, you *should* have an enemy.
>
> When you face your enemy who is going to hurt you, that is the real time to practice toler-

ance. Therefore, an enemy is the cause of the practice of tolerance; tolerance is the effect or result of an enemy. So those are cause and effect. As is said, "Once something has the relationship of arising from that thing, one cannot consider that thing from which it arises as a harmer; rather it assists the production of the effect."

Reflection on this type of reasoning can help develop great patience, which, in turn, develops powerful compassion. Real compassion is based on reason. Ordinary compassion or love is limited by desire or attachment.

If your life is easy and everything is going smoothly, then you can maintain pretenses. However, when you face really desperate situations, there is no time to pretend; you have to deal with reality. Hard times build determination and inner strength. Through them we can also come to appreciate the uselessness of anger. Instead of getting angry, nurture a deep caring and respect for troublemakers because by creating such trying circumstances, they provide us with invaluable opportunities to practice tolerance and patience.

My life has not been a happy time; I have had to pass

through many difficult experiences, including losing my country to Chinese Communist invaders and trying to re-establish our culture in neighboring countries. Yet I regard these difficult periods as among the most important times in my life. Through them, I have gained many new experiences and learned many new ideas—they made me more realistic. When I was young and living high above the city of Lhasa in the Potala Palace, I frequently looked at the life of the city through a telescope. I also learned a lot from the gossip of the sweepers in the palace. They were like my newspaper, relating what the Regent was doing, and what corruption and scandals were going on. I was always happy to listen, and they were proud to be telling the Dalai Lama about what was happening in the streets. The harsh events that unfolded after the invasion in 1950 forced me to become directly involved in issues that otherwise would have been kept at a distance. As a result I have come to prefer a life of committed social action in this world of suffering.

The most difficult time for me was after the Chinese had invaded. I was trying to satisfy the invaders so that the situation would not worsen. When a small delegation of Tibetan officials signed a seventeen-point agreement with the Chinese without the consent of either myself or the government, we were left with no alternative but to attempt to work with the agreement. Many Tibetans resented it, but when they expressed their opposition, the Chinese reacted even more harshly. I was caught in the middle, trying to cool down the situation. The two acting prime ministers on their own complained about the conditions to the Chinese government, which asked me to dismiss them. This is the type of problem I had to face day by day as long as we were in Tibet. We could not concentrate on improving our own situation, but I did set up a reform committee to alleviate excessive charges of interest on debts and so forth.

Against Chinese wishes, I first visited India in 1956 to celebrate the twenty-five hundredth year after Buddha's birth. While in India I had to make the difficult decision of whether to return to Tibet. I was receiving messages about open revolts in eastern Tibet, and many officials in Tibet advised me not to return. Also, from past experience I knew that as China developed more military strength, their attitude would become more harsh. We could see that there was not much hope, but at that time it was not clear that we would have a full guarantee of effective support from the government of India or from another government.

In the end we chose to return to Tibet. But in 1959 when there was a mass escape to India, the situation was easier because the dilemma was gone. We could put all of our energy and time into building a healthy community with modern education for the youth and at the same time try to preserve our traditional ways of studying and practicing Buddhism. We were now working in an atmosphere of freedom without fear.

My own practice has benefited from a life of great turbulence and trouble. You too can come to see the hardships you endure as deepening your practice.

EQUALIZING AND SWITCHING SELF AND OTHER

As Shantideva explains this practice, first you realize that each and every other sentient being wants happiness and does not want suffering, just like you; in this fundamental way you and they are equal. Then, when you consider that you are only a single person measured against an infinite number of other sentient beings, you realize that it would be completely ridiculous either to neglect the welfare of others or to use them for the sake of your own pleasure. It would be far more reasonable to dedicate yourself to their service.

When you consider the situation this way, it becomes very clear. No matter how important you may be, you are only a single person. You have the same right to be happy as everyone else, but the difference is that you are one, and they are many. To lose the happiness of a single person is important, but not so important as losing the happiness of many other beings. From this perspective you can cultivate compassion, love, and respect for others.

In a sense, all human beings belong to a single family. We need to embrace the oneness of humanity and show concern for everyone—not just *my* family or *my* country or *my* continent. We must show concern for every being, not just the few who resemble us. Differences of religion, ideology, race, economic system, social system, and government are all secondary.

Being Wisely Selfish

Put others first; you yourself come next. This works even from a selfish viewpoint. Let me explain how this is possible. You want happiness and do not want suffering, and if you show other people kindness, love, and respect, they will respond in kind; this way your happiness will increase. If you show other people anger and hatred, they will show you the same, and you will lose your own happiness. So I say, if you are selfish, you should be *wisely* selfish. Ordinary selfishness focuses only on your own needs, but if you are wisely selfish, you will treat others just as well as you treat those close to you. Ultimately, this strategy will produce more satisfaction, more happiness. So, even from a selfish viewpoint, you get better results by respecting others, serving others, and reducing self-centeredness.

When you are concerned about others, your own welfare is fulfilled automatically. Consider the physical and verbal nonvirtues, which are causes of being born in a bad situation. Someone with a small outlook avoids killing, for example, out of a motivation to not accumulate a bad karma imprinted in his or her own mind. Someone with a little broader perspective avoids killing by thinking that it will prevent rebirth in a good life where practice in order to leave the entire round of cyclic existence could be continued. However, altruistic people consider others' lives to be as important as their own and avoid murder out of wanting to protect another person's life. This cherishing of others makes a huge difference in the strength of the motivation to refrain from killing. Those whose motivation is self-centered could think that even if they commit such an ill-deed, they could confess and seek to ameliorate the karma, whereas someone who values another person's life cares about the other's suffering and knows that it would not help that person to confess to murder. The same is true for stealing, adultery, lying, divisive talk, harsh speech, and even, I think, senseless chatter.

Another way that other-concern is so valuable is that it puts your own situation in perspective. At one point I was particularly saddened about the situation of Tibet, but then I remembered that I had taken the Bodhi-sattva vows and every day frequently reflected on Shan-tideva's prayer:

> As long as the sky exists
> And as long as there are sentient beings,
> May I remain to help
> Relieve them of all their pain.

As soon as I remembered this, the whole feeling of burden immediately cleared away, much like heavy clothes being lifted off me.

Altruistic commitment relieves specific causes of dejection by placing them in a broader perspective; these causes should not discourage you. Most of one's own troubles, worries, and sadness in this life comes from self-cherishing. As I mentioned above, being wisely selfish is not negative, but short-sighted selfishness, concerned only with immediate satisfaction, is counterproductive. A narrow perspective makes even a small problem unbearable. Being concerned about all sentient beings widens your view, making you more realistic. In this way an altruistic attitude helps to reduce your own pain right now.

My earnest request is that you practice love and kindness whether you believe in a religion or not. Through this practice you will come to realize the value of compassion and kindness for your own peace of mind. After all, even though you may not be concerned with other people, you are very much concerned with yourself—no question about it—so you must want to achieve a peaceful mind and a happier daily life. If you practice more kindness and tolerance, you will find more peace. There is no need to change the furniture in your house or move to a new home. Your neighbor may be very noisy or very difficult, but so long as your own mind is calm and peaceful, neighbors will not bother you much. However, if you are generally irritable, even when your best friend visits, you cannot become really happy. If you are calm, even your enemy cannot disturb you.

This is why I say that if you are really selfish, you are better off being wisely selfish. This way you can fulfill your selfish motive to be happy. That is much better than being self-centered, or foolishly selfish, which will not succeed.

Visualization

The following visualization technique is very helpful in daily practice.

1. You remain calm and reasonable.
2. In front of you to the right, imagine another version of yourself who is a solid mass of egotistical self-centeredness, the kind of person who would do anything to satisfy an urge.
3. In front of you to the left, visualize a group of poor people who are not related to you, including some who are destitute, needy, suffering.
4. Be calm and unbiased as you observe these two sides.

Now think, "Both want happiness. Both want to shed suffering. Both have the right to accomplish these goals."

5. Consider this: We often work long and hard for a better salary, or we spend a great deal of money in hopes of gaining even more; we are willing to make temporary sacrifices for a long-term return. By the same logic, it makes perfect sense for one single person to make sacrifices in order to help a larger good. Naturally your mind will favor the side with the greater number of suffering people.

As an unbiased observer, consider your own egotistical self there at your right side, neglecting the welfare of so many, no matter how terrible their suffering. It simply is not good to be like this. Though both sides that you are visualizing have an equal right to happiness, there is no way to avoid the overwhelming need of the greater number. The point is that you yourself must serve and help other beings.

This state of mind is undeniably difficult, but if you practice it with great determination, then year by year, your mind will change, will improve. In the mid-sixties I gave a teaching on Tsongkhapa's *Stages of the Path to Enlightenment,* during which I mentioned that if I achieved the first level of true cessation of afflictive emotions, I would take a long rest. I really felt that way. Even though I admired altruism, I thought it would be too difficult to develop. Then around 1967 I received teaching on Shantideva's *A Guide to the Bodhisattva Way of Life* from the Kagyu Lama Kunu Tenzin Gyeltsen and began to reflect more on its meaning, along with Nagarjuna's *Precious Garland.* Eventually I gained some confidence that with enough time I could develop this high degree of compassion. Now, beginning from around 1970, every morning when I contemplate altruism, I cry. This is how transformation takes place. I do not claim to have developed a high degree of altruism, but I am confident that I can.

Even if your experience of altruistic motivation is modest, it will definitely give you a degree of mental peace. Generating concern for others has vast power to transform your mind. If you practice compassion for the sake of all living beings—including animals—then that same limitless merit will accrue to you.

Realizing Our Responsibility

Even if you cannot, for the time being, rise to the level of cherishing others more than yourself, at least you can begin to see that it is not right to neglect others. We have a human body and the power of human judgment, but if we use these only for our own self-centered ends, and not for the sake of others, we are no better than animals. In fact ants, to cite just one example, work unselfishly for the community; we humans sometimes do not look good by comparison. We are supposed to be higher beings, so we must act according to our higher selves.

If we look at world history, most great tragedies that involved terrible loss of life were brought about by human beings. Humans make the mess. Today millions of people live in constant fear of racial, ethnic, and economic conflict. Who is responsible for this fear? Not animals. The consequences of war include the deaths of many animals, but this does not bother us; we are solely concerned with ourselves. There is much talk about stopping war, but we must go beyond wishful thinking. What is our human value when we live with no show of compassion, no show of concern, just killing and eating animals, and fighting and killing thousands of people? It is our responsibility to clean up the mess.

Nowadays, one of the best ways to communicate is through television. People who work in television and wish to practice this noble idea of caring for others could make a substantial contribution. Although stories of lust and murder provide exciting entertainment, they have negative influences deep in the mind. We do not need this kind of entertainment all the time—although this is probably none of my business!

We must educate our young children in the practice of compassion. Teachers and parents can instill in children real, warmhearted human values to tremendous benefit. I noticed in a newspaper that a toy company which usually makes toy rifles and so forth deliberately stopped producing violent toys at Christmas. What a wonderful idea! What an other-centered act!

DECIDING TO ACHIEVE ENLIGHTENMENT

Once you get to the point of deeply wanting to do whatever is possible to relieve suffering and uproot its causes, and to help all beings achieve happiness and its causes, reflect on how this could be brought about. It can only happen if other people also come to understand how this works, and then implement those practices. Therefore, your commitment to the highest welfare of other beings can best be supported by teaching them how to practice and what behavior to forsake, so that they themselves can have the power to attain happiness and avoid suffering. There is no other way. For this to happen, you yourself must know their inner dispositions and interests as well as what to teach them.

Thus, for the sake of helping others, you should be fully prepared. What is that preparation? You have to remove all obstacles in your own mind to knowing everything that can be known. What compassionate practitioners—called Bodhisattvas—really want is not just to overcome the obstructions which prevent their own liberation; they want to clear the way to omniscience so that they can gain access to other people's dispositions and discern which techniques will help them. If it were simply a matter of choice, the Bodhisattvas would choose to remove the obstructions to omniscience first. However, the afflictive emotions (keeping us trapped in cyclic existence) establish the obstructions to omniscience, which are predispositions in the mind causing phenomena to *appear* as if they are inherently existent. Without first overcoming the chief afflictive emotion—the ignorance that *believes* in inherent existence—you cannot overcome the predispositions deposited in the mind by that ignorance. Through purification of the afflictive obstructions as well as the predispositions established by them, you can transform your own consciousness into the omniscient consciousness of a Buddha, full enlightenment.

To sum up, to bring about the complete happiness of others it is necessary to become enlightened yourself. When you understand this and resolve to seek enlightenment for their sake, this is called the altruistic intention toward enlightenment, or *bodhichitta*. By following Shantideva's practice of seeing self and others as equally striving for happiness and then switching the emphasis on your own aims over to those of infinite others, you can generate the power of *bodhichitta* within you.

There are three different styles of altruistic attitude found in three types of people. The first type is like a monarch, desiring to achieve Buddhahood first, as the most effective way to help other beings. The second is like a boatman, desiring to arrive at the other shore of enlightenment together with all other beings. The third is like a shepherd, desiring that all others should achieve Buddhahood first, before his or her own enlightenment.

The last two analogies only indicate the compassionate attitude of certain types of practitioners; in actuality there is no case like the boatman, of everyone attaining enlightenment simultaneously, nor like the shepherd, prior to oneself. Rather, enlightenment always comes in the first way, like a monarch, since Bodhisattvas eventually decide to become enlightened as fast as possible so that they can more effectively help others on a vast scale. As the Tibetan sage Sakya Pandita says in his *Differentiation of the Three Vows,* Bodhisattvas have two kinds of prayer-wishes, those that can be accomplished and those that cannot. In Shantideva's *A Guide to the Bodhisattva Way of Life* there are many examples of wishes that cannot actually be achieved but are there for the sake of developing strong will and determination. For example, the practice of giving away your own happiness and taking the suffering of others upon yourself is not literally possible, except perhaps for minor forms of suffering. Just as this practice, though unrealistic, is intended to increase the courage of compassion, the analogies of the boatman and shepherd serve to indicate how powerfully Bodhisattvas wish to help others.

Let me give an example of this dedication that has been brought to the level of profound experience. There was a scholarly practitioner from the Drashikyil monastery in the northeastern province of Tibet called Amdo. In 1950 when the Chinese Communists invaded and arrested one thousand out of the three thousand monks at the monastery, a hundred of them were marked to be killed. He was one of them. Taken to execution grounds, and just before being shot, he prayed:

> May all the ill deeds, obstructions, and
> sufferings of beings
> Be transferred to me, without exception,
> at this moment,
> And my happiness and merit be sent to
> others.
> May all creatures be imbued with happi-
> ness!

Just a few moments before being killed, he had the spiritual presence to remember the practice of taking on others' pain and giving away his own happiness! It is easy to talk about such practice when things are going well, but he was able to implement it at the hardest of times. This is a clear indication of spiritual attainment acquired from long practice.

As Shantideva's *A Guide to the Bodhisattva Way of Life* says, if a blind person finds a jewel in a pile of garbage, she would cherish it dearly. If, in the midst of the garbage of lust, hatred, and ignorance—emotions that afflict our own minds and our world—we generate a compassionate attitude, we should cherish this like a jewel. This precious discovery can give us happiness and real tranquility. Alternatives such as taking a vacation or drugs only bring temporary relief. A disciplined attitude of true other-concern, in which you cherish others more than yourself, is helpful both to you and to others. It does no harm to anyone, temporarily or in the long run. Compassion is a priceless jewel.

Care about others at all times. If you cannot help others, do no harm. This is the essential meaning of the practice of morality.

SUMMARY FOR DAILY PRACTICE

On a daily basis, perform the visualization in five steps described earlier:

1. Remain calm and reasonable.
2. In front of you to the right, imagine another version of yourself, egotistical and self-centered.
3. In front of you to the left, imagine a group of poor people, suffering beings who are unrelated to you, neither friend nor enemy.
4. Observe these two sides from your calm vantage point. Now think, "Both want happiness. Both want to get rid of suffering. Both have the right to accomplish these goals."
5. Consider this: Just as usually we are willing to make temporary sacrifices for a greater long-term good, so too the benefit of the larger number of suffering beings to your left is much more important than this single egotistical person on your right. Notice your mind naturally turning to the side of the greater number of people.

6

Aspiring to Enlightenment

❖

WHY SEEK ENLIGHTENMENT?

Compassion is the key to achieving a deeper level of morality, yet how can we help others when we ourselves are beset by wrong attitudes? Without being in a better position ourselves, it is difficult for us to help others on the large scale we have been discussing. For example, if you are going to help people who are illiterate, you have to be educated. Similarly, to help so many sentient beings we must achieve Buddhahood, since a Buddha has all the qualities necessary to help them—knowledge of all the techniques for spiritual development and clairvoyant knowledge of their emotions, interests, dispositions, and so forth. When you are moved through the practice of compassion to feel concern for others, it is time for new values to take root. We prepare the ground of our mind for these new values by engaging in the ritual for aspiring to enlightenment.

You are already equipped with the basic qualities needed to attain complete enlightenment—the luminous and cognitive nature of your mind. Therefore, focus on the thought, "I will attain unsurpassed perfect enlightenment for the sake of sentient beings throughout limitless space." Nurture this intention until it is strong. The ritual for aspiring to altruistic enlightenment is very helpful in this process.

SEVEN MERITORIOUS PRACTICES

This ritual, which should become part of your daily meditation, begins with seven steps followed by a special offering. These practices increase your force of merit, which in turn leads you more surely to transformation. Through these forms of devotion you will intensify your commitment to compassion; as you see below, they all involve paying devotion to those special beings who teach compassion.

1. *Homage.* Imagine Shakyamuni Buddha surrounded by innumerable Bodhisattvas, filling the sky in front of you, and pay homage with your body, speech, and mind. Put your palms together, and feel intensely that you are respectfully taking refuge in the Buddhas and Bodhisattvas. Say out loud, "Homage to Shakyamuni Buddha and the Bodhisattvas."

2. *Offering.* Spread out offerings, such as fruit or incense. Imagine everything that might be suitable to be offered—whether you own it or not—including your body, your resources, and your own virtue. Then imagine offering these in their entirety to the Buddhas and Bodhisattvas.

3. *Disclosing ill deeds.* We have all been responsible for countless ill deeds of body, speech, and mind motivated by the desire to do harm. In the spirit of full disclosure, develop a sense of regret for having done them, as if through those actions you had eaten poison. Generate, too, an intention to abstain from these actions in the future as if to

do otherwise might cost you your life. Think, "From the bottom of my heart, I disclose to the Buddhas and Bodhisattvas the ill deeds that I have done." The main way to purify bad deeds is through regret. The greater your regret, the stronger your intention not to repeat them in the future.

4. *Admiration.* From the depths of your heart admire your own virtuous actions and those of others. Take joy in the good things you have done in this lifetime. Focus on specific good deeds such as giving to a charity. The fact that you have a human body in this lifetime and the opportunity to practice altruism is evidence of virtuous actions in past lives. So take joy in those virtues, too, and think to yourself, "I really did something good." Also take joy in the virtues of others, whether you have seen them firsthand or not. Take joy in the innumerable virtues of the Buddhas and Bodhisattvas over limitless time. By delighting in your own virtues and those of others, you will keep from regretting your own virtuous deeds (wishing you had not given to a charity because it caused your bank account to dwindle, for example) and you will also avoid

becoming jealous of the good deeds of others, or competitive with them.

5. *Entreaty.* Ask the Buddhas who have become completely enlightened but have not yet engaged in teaching spiritual doctrine, to do so on behalf of all who suffer.

6. *Supplication.* Pray to the Buddhas not to pass away. This is a specific request for Buddhas who have taught and are nearing the time to pass away.

7. *Dedication.* Rather than directing your practice of the previous steps toward temporary happiness and comfort in this lifetime or the next, or to merely becoming liberated from cyclic existence, dedicate it toward attaining highest enlightenment. Think, "May these acts help me attain full and perfect enlightenment for the sake of all sentient beings."

Then imagine that the entire world system has been purified and offer it with all conceivable marvels to the Buddhas and Bodhisattvas. This special offering nourishes compassion by offering all things desirable to those who teach it.

COMMITTING TO HELP

Now you are ready for the actual ritual of aspiring to enlightenment for the care of others. It comes in two parts, the first of which is the recitation of a short statement of refuge: "Until I reach enlightenment I seek refuge in Buddha, the doctrine, and the supreme spiritual community." In its most compassionate form, refuge is the union of three attitudes:

1. Concern for the state of suffering of all beings, not just for yourself. Concern, too, that they not seek mere solitary relief from suffering but aspire to the altruistic enlightenment of Buddhahood.
2. Faith in the Buddha, the states of realization, and the spiritual community, maintaining the conviction that through them all beings will find freedom from all suffering.
3. Compassion, which means not being able to stand the enslavement of others to suffering without doing something about it.

Know that the Buddha is the teacher of refuge, that the true paths and true cessations are the actual refuge, and that the Bodhisattvas who have directly realized the true nature of phenomena are our spiritual community, leading all sentient beings to refuge.

With that knowledge, aspire to highest enlightenment by reciting: "Through the collections of merit of my giving, morality, patience, effort, concentration, and wisdom, may I achieve Buddhahood in order to help all beings." As you do, think to yourself, "Through the force of these, may I achieve Buddhahood not to help myself but to be of service to all sentient beings in order to help them reach Buddhahood." This is called generation of a compassionate intention to become enlightened in the form of a wish.

This brings us to the central part of the ritual. With a strong wish to attain Buddhahood in order to serve other beings, imagine before you a Buddha or your own spiritual teacher as a representative of him.

I. Recite the following as if you were repeating it after the Buddha:

> Until I reach enlightenment I seek refuge in Buddha, the doctrine, and the supreme spiritual community.

Through the collections of merit of my giving, morality, patience, effort, concentration, and wisdom, may I achieve Buddhahood in order to help all beings.

By saying this you are directing your virtuous actions not to some small purpose in this life, or the next, but to the greatest purpose of all—the attainment of total freedom for all beings. Generate this attitude with great determination.

2. Make the second repetition with even stronger resolve to make this altruistic goal a constant in your day-to-day life:

Until I reach enlightenment I seek refuge in Buddha, the doctrine, and the supreme spiritual community.

Through the collections of merit of my giving, morality, patience, effort, concentration, and wisdom, may I achieve Buddhahood in order to help all beings.

3. Make the third repetition with even greater determination, from the depths of your heart. Make a lasting, fully reasoned decision—unshake-

able by circumstance—that the welfare of so many others is far greater than your own. Think, "Now when I have such a great opportunity, what could be more important than striving for the benefit of others! From now on, to the full extent of my ability, I will stop concentrating on my own welfare and will commit myself deeply to the advancement of all beings. To accomplish this, I will achieve unsurpassed perfect enlightenment." Recite:

Until I reach enlightenment I seek refuge in Buddha, the doctrine, and the supreme spiritual community.

Through the collections of merit of my giving, morality, patience, effort, concentration, and wisdom, may I achieve Buddhahood in order to help all beings.

This concludes the ritual. Through it you plant and nurture the seeds of strong and unwavering compassion.

MAINTAINING COMMITMENT IN THIS LIFETIME

There are four practices aimed at keeping this altruism from deteriorating in this lifetime:

1. First, increase your enthusiasm for becoming enlightened for the sake of others by recalling again and again the benefits of doing so.

2. Then, increase your concern for others by dividing the day and night into three periods each, and during those periods take a little time from your day, or rouse yourself from sleep, to practice the five-step visualization given on page 84, even for just five minutes. This practice is very effective; it becomes a regular habit, like eating food at a certain time. If you cannot do this so often, visualize the steps three times in one morning session that lasts around fifteen minutes, and do the same at night. Ponder the meaning of your aim: "May I attain highest enlightenment for others!"

3. The next practice requires vigilance: In seeking to gain highest enlightenment for the sake of *all* beings, make sure not to mentally neglect the welfare of even one.

4. Try to accumulate the two forces of merit and wisdom as much as possible. To increase merit, engage willingly in virtuous activities like generosity and morality. To accumulate wisdom, you must come to understand the true way phenomena exist. Since this is a complicated topic, we will be exploring it at length in Chapters Eight–Ten. Suffice it to say here that it is helpful to reflect on how phenomena arise and exist dependent on causes and conditions.

MAINTAINING COMMITMENT IN FUTURE LIFETIMES

In future lifetimes your compassionate intention to become enlightened could weaken. You can prevent this from happening by abandoning the four unwholesome activities listed below, and by training in the four wholesome practices that follow them.

Four Unwholesome Practices

1. Deceiving a high person such as an abbot, ordination master, lama, or fellow practitioner about negative things that you have done.

2. Causing others engaged in virtue to regret what they are doing.

3. Criticizing or belittling those who express compassion for others.

4. Deceit and misrepresentation to get others' services.

Four Wholesome Practices

1. Do not lie to anyone at all. There are exceptions, when lying can result in great benefit to others, but they are rare.

2. Help others move toward the altruistic enlightenment of Buddhahood, directly or indirectly.

3. Consider and treat Bodhisattvas with the same respect as Buddha. Since we do not know who is and who is not a Bodhisattva, we must treat all beings with respect. As a general rule, place others above you.

4. Never cheat anyone and always remain honest.

If you have the resolve to train in these practices to generate a determination to achieve Buddhahood for others, then make this *promise:* "I will maintain my determination and never give it up." Those who cannot maintain this level of training can forgo the promise and instead can think, "May I attain highest enlightenment for the sake of all beings!" People who are not Buddhists—Christians, Jews, Moslems, and so forth— can generate an other-concerned attitude of equal value by thinking, "I will bring about help and happiness for all beings."

PRACTICAL INTENTION TO BECOME ENLIGHTENED

When your aspiration to become enlightened is firm, you should implement it in deeds. These are called Bodhisattva deeds, and principal among them are the six perfections:

1. *Giving* includes (1) donating material things such as money, clothing, and food; (2) giving love; (3) giving the teachings of spiritual doctrines and practices; and (4) giving relief from fearful situations to all beings—including animals; help even an ant out of a puddle

2. *Morality,* which refers mainly to the altruistic attitude and behavior of Bodhisattvas

3. *Patience,* which is exhibited in stressful situations, or used to sustain difficult endeavors, such as learning teachings and practicing over a long period

4. *Effort,* which maintains enthusiasm for virtue and assists all the other perfections

5. *Concentration,* which is the practice of stable and intense meditation explained in the next chapter

6. *Wisdom,* which is necessary for understanding the nature of cyclic existence and impermanence, as well as dependent-arising and emptiness

The six perfections, in turn, can be condensed into the three trainings of Bodhisattvas—training in the perfection of morality (which includes the perfections of giving and patience), training in the perfection of concentration, and training in the perfection of wisdom. The perfection of effort is required for all three trainings. This is how the six perfections are included in the three-fold practice of morality, concentrated meditation, and wisdom that is the focus of this book.

When you arrive at the feeling in the depths of your heart that you must engage in Bodhisattva deeds—these being the six perfections or, seen another way, the three-fold practice—this is the appropriate time to take the Bodhisattva vows of the *practical* intention to become enlightened.

❖

In essence, all beings are united by the desire to gain happiness and avoid suffering. We are also the same in that it is possible to remove suffering and attain happiness, to which we all have an equal right. Then what is the difference between you and all others? You are a minority of one. It is easy to see that the vast number of sentient beings hoping for happiness and seeking an end to suffering are more important than any one person. It is therefore eminently reasonable for you to commit yourself to the welfare of innumerable others, to use your body, speech, and mind for their good, and to abandon an attitude of just taking care of yourself.

❖

SUMMARY FOR DAILY PRACTICE

First take the seven preliminary steps:

1. *Pay homage* to Shakyamuni Buddha surrounded by innumerable Bodhisattvas, whom you imagine filling the sky before you.
2. *Offer* all wonderful things—whether you own them or not—including your body, your resources, and your own virtue, to the Buddhas and Bodhisattvas.
3. *Disclose* the countless ill deeds of body, speech, and mind you have perpetrated with an intent to harm others. Regret having done them, and resolve to abstain from them in the future.
4. *Admire* from the depths of the heart your own virtues and those of others. Take joy in the good things you have done in this and previous lives, thinking, "I have done something good." Take joy in the virtues of others, including those of Buddhas and Bodhisattvas.
5. *Entreat* the Buddhas who have become completely enlightened but have not yet taught, to teach for the sake of those who suffer.

6. *Supplicate* the Buddhas not to pass away.
7. *Dedicate* these six practices to attaining highest enlightenment.

Then undertake the central part of the ritual for aspiring to enlightenment:

1. With a strong determination to attain Buddhahood in order to serve other beings, imagine a Buddha in front of you, or your spiritual teacher as a representative of Buddha.
2. Recite three times as if you are repeating after him or her:

> Until I reach enlightenment I seek refuge in Buddha, the doctrine, and the supreme spiritual community.
>
> Through the collections of merit of my giving, morality, patience, effort, concentration, and wisdom, may I achieve Buddhahood in order to help all beings.

To maintain and strengthen this profound altruism in this life perform the following:

1. Recall again and again the benefits of developing an intention to become enlightened for the sake of others.

2. Divide the day into three periods and the night into three periods, and during each of those periods take a little time out or rouse yourself from sleep and practice the five-step visualization given in the last chapter. It is also sufficient to visualize the five steps three times in one morning session that lasts around fifteen minutes, and three times in one night session for fifteen minutes.

3. Avoid mentally neglecting the welfare of even one being.

4. As much as possible, engage in virtuous activity with a good attitude, and develop a rough understanding of the nature of reality, or maintain a wish to do so and work at it.

To maintain and strengthen this profound altruism in future lives:

1. Do not lie to anyone at all, unless you can help others greatly through lying.

2. Directly or indirectly help people to progress toward enlightenment.
3. Treat all beings with respect.
4. Never cheat anyone, and always remain honest.

In essence, think again and again, "May I become able to help all beings."

III

PRACTICING CONCENTRATED MEDITATION

7

Focusing the Mind

❖

Let us take a moment to review how progress toward a meaningful life unfolds: First comes morality, then concentrated meditation, then wisdom. Wisdom relies on the single-mindedness of meditation, and meditation depends upon the self-awareness of morality. In the last five chapters we have discussed the practice of morality, which makes you more settled and peaceful and your mind ready for more spiritual advancement. With a conscious mode of behavior, concentrated meditation, called calm abiding, can be accomplished. Still, your mind is too scattered for increasingly effective meditative practice which requires full concentration. Even a small noise here or there can immediately distract you. Since it is absolutely necessary to make the mind much more focused so that wisdom can take hold, I will discuss in this chapter the process of developing the profoundly concentrated state of calm abiding. First I will briefly describe the various types of meditation so that you can understand the place that calm abiding takes among them.

TYPES OF MEDITATION

There are many ways to meditate.

- Two basic types of meditation are *analytical meditation* and *stabilizing meditation.* In analytical meditation you analyze a topic trying to understand it through reasoning. For instance, you might meditate on why things are impermanent by reflecting on how they are produced by causes or how they disintegrate moment by moment. In stabilizing meditation you fix your mind on a single object or topic, such as impermanence. (Calm abiding is cultivated through stabilizing meditation.)
- Another way of dividing meditation is between *subjective meditation* and *objective meditation.* In subjective

meditation your aim is to cultivate in the mind a new, or strengthened perspective, or attitude. The cultivation of faith is an example of this type of meditation; faith is not the object *on* which you are concentrating but an attitude that is being meditatively cultivated. (Cultivation of compassion is subjective meditation because you are not meditating *on* compassion but seeking to make your consciousness more compassionate.) In objective meditation you meditate *on* a topic, such as on impermanence, or an object, such as on the golden body of a Buddha.

♦ You can *meditate in the manner of wishing.* For example, you might wish to be filled with the compassion and wisdom of a Buddha.

♦ Or, you can go one step further, into *imaginative meditation* in which you envision that you have qualities that you actually do not yet have. The practice of deity yoga, for example, calls for meditating on yourself as an ideal being whose body is made from the light of wisdom.

Of these various forms of meditation let us discuss how to practice the stabilizing meditation of calm abiding. As mentioned above, the aim of stabilizing meditation is to strengthen the mind's ability to focus on a single object or topic, which in turn enables the mind to overcome problems at their root. It will also help you to be more alert and sharp in daily life; it will gradually increase your power of memory, which is useful in all parts of your life.

ACHIEVING CALM ABIDING

Since in this type of meditation you are seeking to achieve a deeply concentrated state of mind you need the following:

1. The *initial cause,* morality, which brings you a peaceful, relaxed, conscientious mode of behavior and thus removes coarse distractions.

2. A *time and place for practice* apart from the commotion of daily life. Make time for meditation in your daily schedule. For focused meditation, being alone in a secluded, quiet spot is crucial. Since noise is the thorn preventing concentration, at the beginning it is very important to stay in a quiet place. Consider taking a retreat for your vacation.

3. A suitable *diet* fostering clarity of mind. For some health conditions, it may be necessary to eat meat, but, generally speaking, vegetarian food is best. According to the morality of individual liberation, there is no prohibition against eating meat on occasion. But you should not eat meat that is purposely killed for you, and you should not ask for it if it is not offered. Indeed, it would be most welcome if the majority of people did become vegetarian. Some Great Vehicle scriptures prohibit the eating of meat, since concern for others is the heart of Great Vehicle morality. Also, eating too much food is not good, so eat less. Of course, drinking alcohol is out of the question, as are all mind-altering drugs. Smoking is not advisable. If a bearded man was smoking while entering into deep meditation, he would risk having his beard catch on fire!

4. The right amount of *sleep.* Too much makes your mind dull, and too little can be disruptive. You have to figure out what the right amount is for you.

5. *Physical posture* is critical to focused meditation, especially at this early stage. If possible, assume the full- or half-lotus position. Use two cushions, putting a smaller one under your rear so that your rear is higher

than your knees, the effect being that no matter how much you meditate you will not be as likely to become tired. Straighten your backbone like an arrow; bend your head just a little downward; aim your eyes over the nose to the front; put your tongue against the roof of the mouth; leave your lips and teeth as usual; and leave your arms a little loose, not forcing them against the body. With regard to positioning the hands, Japanese Zen practitioners usually put the left hand, palm up, on top of the right, which is also palm up. Tibetans put the right hand, palm up, on top of the left, which is also palm up. In Tantric practice it is important to put the right hand on top of the left, with both palms up, and with the two thumbs pressed together in the form of a triangle, the base of which is about four finger-widths below the navel.

The Object of Meditation

There are many possible objects of the stabilizing meditation for achieving calm abiding:

◆ The breath. Some texts speak of watching the inhalation and exhalation of breath through the nose but do not address the topic of how deep to breathe. Other texts explain how to imagine the movement of breath in specific areas in the body. In one type of breathing exercise, you pull up the lower airs, or energies, and press down the upper energies, holding them as if in a vessel just below the navel.

- Your body, feelings, mind, or phenomena such as impermanence. These meditations are called establishments through mindfulness.

- The first letter of your name on a disc of light outside or inside your body.

- In Thailand practitioners often meditate within applying mindfulness to whatever they do. While walking they are mindful of putting the right foot forward, then the left, then the right.

- In general a good object of meditation for a Buddhist is an image of the body of Shakyamuni Buddha; for a Christian it could be an image of Jesus. Gaze at it so that it appears to your mind internally when you close your eyes. Meditate on the figure at eye level, not too high or low, at a distance of about four or five feet.

At the beginning it is difficult to get the object of meditation to appear clearly in your mind. To avoid dulling your perception, try frequent, intense five-minute sessions rather than long meditations. (Four to sixteen of these brief sessions daily is ideal.) When it finally appears internally, you have found your object of meditation. Now fix your mind continuously upon it.

Counteracting Excitement and Laxity

To achieve calm abiding, both stability and clarity are needed with respect to the object of meditation. Thus the biggest obstacles to sustained meditation are excitement and laxity. Excitement prevents stability. When the mind does not stay on the object but becomes distracted or scattered, the object of meditation is lost. There is also a subtle form of excitement, where even if the object is not lost, a corner of the mind is thinking about something else. You need to identify excitement and, through mindfulness, not let your mind come under its influence.

Lethargy, a heaviness of mind and body, is an obstacle to clarity. Lethargy also causes laxity, which prevents clarity. In coarse laxity the mind sinks; the object of meditation fades and is lost. In subtle laxity, the object is not lost, but the clarity of the object and of the mind diminish a little because the mind's intensity has weakened; the mind is a little too loose. The mind might stay quite clearly on the object of meditation, but without true alertness; this state is often mistaken for proper meditation.

When your mind is too intense, and you experience excitement, you need to loosen it, like loosening the strings of a guitar a bit. Similarly, when you have laxity, your mind is not intense enough, so you need to increase its intensity by making it a little more taut, like tightening the strings. As you see, the mind needs to be tuned like a fine stringed instrument.

Mindfulness and Introspection

The force behind developing concentrated meditation is mindfulness, which is the ability to stay with an object, not allowing distraction. You exercise mindfulness by putting your mind back on its object of meditation every time it falters, which will happen again and again. When you become skilled in maintaining mindfulness on the object, you need to use introspection. As

Shantideva's *A Guide to the Bodhisattva Way of Life* says, the special function of introspection is periodically to inspect your activities, whether physical or mental. In the process of developing calm abiding, the task of introspection is to determine whether the mind has come, or is about to come, under the influence of laxity or excitement. At the start, periods of laxity and excitement are strong, but, with effort, these become weaker and less frequent, and the periods of being able to stay on the object lengthen. Gradually, even subtle laxity and excitement lose their force and disappear. Ultimately, the ability of the mind to stay one-pointedly on the object, free from the faults of excitement and laxity, increases.

When through mindfulness and introspection you can sustain the continuum of holding the object, it is possible to achieve concentrated meditation within six months. Initially you must forcibly put your mind on the object of meditation with great exertion; then from time to time you engage the object without great exertion; then you engage it in a relaxed way continuously; and finally you spontaneously stay on the object without needing to make any effort to remove excitement and laxity. If you are able to remain on your object for four hours vividly and continuously, you have achieved firm stability. Unfavorable states of body and mind are gone, and a bliss of physical and mental pliancy is attained. At that point, you have achieved calm abiding.

Qualities of Calm Abiding

To be endowed with calm abiding, the mind must have the *stability* to hold fast to one object, but this alone is not sufficient. The mind must also be *clear,* but this, too, is not enough. Its clarity should be *intense, alert,* and *sharp*; the mind cannot be even a little dull.

These fine adjustments to the mind to make it susceptible to calm abiding are not easily accomplished. In Dharamsala, India, one of the Tibetans practicing concentrated meditation told me that the cultivation of one-pointed concentration was worse than imprisonment in a Chinese jail! Because it is difficult, it is important to prepare carefully, moving from step to step. Do not push yourself too hard, especially at first, otherwise you run the risk of becoming upset or even having a nervous breakdown. The goal here is daily practice, where you choose an object of meditation, and as you focus on it, try to achieve and maintain stability, clarity, and intensity.

Concentrating on the Mind Itself

Calm abiding can also be achieved through daily meditations on the mind itself. One of the advantages of observing the mind now is that it will strengthen your ability to manifest the mind of clear light as you are dying. First identify the mind's essential nature of luminosity and knowing, unsullied by thought, and then concentrate on it. This is one among many levels of thoughtlessness (I will describe meditation on the ultimate nature of the mind in Chapter Ten).

To prepare for concentrating on the mind itself you need to overcome emotional obstacles by engaging in the accumulation of positive merit, such as through developing compassion as discussed earlier. The next step is to become familiar with the nature of your own mind. The best time for this is early in the morning, just after waking up, but before all your sense faculties have become active. Your eyes are not yet open. Look at, or within, consciousness itself. This is a good opportunity to experience the clear light nature of the mind. Do not let your mind think on what has happened in the past, nor let it chase after things that might happen in the future; rather, leave the mind vivid, without any constructions, just as it is. In the space between old and new ideas, discover the natural, unfabricated, luminous and knowing nature of the mind unaffected by thought. When you remain this way, you understand that the mind is like a mirror, reflecting any object, any conception, and that the mind has a nature of mere luminosity and knowing, of mere experience.

After you recognize the nature of the mind as luminosity and knowing, stay with it. Using your powers of mindfulness and introspection remain in that state. If a thought comes, just look into its very nature, and the concept will lose its power and dissolve of its own accord. Sometimes, with exertion, you can prevent a thought from fully forming. More likely, though, when you reach this state of recognizing the basic, unaffected, unfabricated nature of the mind, thoughts will dissolve as they form, and even when they do come, they will not be powerful. Know that just as the waves of the ocean are made of water, thoughts are made of the luminous, knowing nature of the mind. And through continual daily practice, thoughts will weaken and disappear without any other exertion.

This practice of meditation itself sharpens your mind and improves your memory, qualities that are certainly useful beyond spiritual practice, whether in business, engineering, raising a family, or being a teacher, doctor, or lawyer. This practice also helps on a daily basis with anger. When you get irritated, you can concentrate on the nature of the anger itself and thereby undermine its force.

Another benefit of such mental training emerges from the close connection between body and mind. When you are young and physically fit, your mind is powerful. It is particularly valuable to begin training then, so that as you age, your mind stays fresh and positive through the body's changes. After all, the human brain is a special endowment, and it would be a pity to let it weaken through neglect, surrendering its powers to age until, animallike, its only job is to take care of the body. For practitioners, early mental training, and especially concentration on the mind, is important preparation for the final day, when your mind must remain clear and sharp to make use of special techniques during the stages of death or at least to influence rebirth into the next life. Dullness of mind at this critical point can be very dangerous. A real guarantee for a good rebirth is to be able to conduct your practice during the stages of dying.

Your state of mind just before rebirth is influential in determining the character of your next life. You may have accumulated great merit in your life, but if you leave it with a dull mind, you jeopardize the form that your next life will take. On the other hand, even if you committed some regrettable deeds in your lifetime, when the final day comes, if you are prepared and determined to use that occasion to the fullest, your next rebirth will definitely be good. Therefore, strive to train the mind to be fresh, alert, and sharp.

OTHER TECHNIQUES FOR ACHIEVING MENTAL CALM

In difficult situations it is easy to become emotionally worked up. Buddhism offers many techniques for relieving stress and finding calm in the trying situations we face every day. These techniques vary according to the situation and the person. It is particularly effective to use the power of analytical meditation to address problems directly, rather than trying to avoid them. Here are some examples of this technique.

♦ When you are confronted with trouble, do whatever you can to overcome it, but if it is insurmountable, then reflect on the fact that this trouble is due to your own actions in this, or a previous, life. Understanding that suffering comes from karma will bring some peace as it reveals that life is not unjust. Otherwise sorrow and pain might seem to be meaningless.

◆ Initially a problem can seem solid and intractable, until you investigate its true nature. To do this, work at understanding the range of suffering in your own life. Ordinary mind and body have a nature of suffering, just as it is the nature of fire to be hot and burning. In the same way we have learned how to work with the nature of fire, we can learn how to work with suffering in our lives.

◆ Consider trouble from a broader perspective. If someone accuses you, rather than lashing out, imagine that this accusation loosens the chains of your own self-cherishing, and thereby enhances your ability to care for others. Reframe bad circumstances as forces assisting your spiritual development. This technique is difficult to implement but very powerful when you succeed.

◆ When you are jealous or wish harm on an enemy, instead of stewing over that person's bad qualities, reflect on his or her attributes. Most people are a mixture of good and bad qualities—it is hard to find anyone who is bad in all respects.

- Reflect on the emptiness of inherent existence—this is the deepest analytical meditation and something I will explore in the next three chapters.

Or, you can use stabilizing meditation for a temporary rest:

- If you cannot stop worrying over something in the past or what might happen in the future, shift your focus to the inhalation and exhalation of your breath. Or recite this mantra: *om mani padme hum* (pronounced "om mani padmay hum"). Since the mind cannot concentrate on two things simultaneously, either of these meditations causes the former worry to fade.

It seems to me that all religions could benefit from Buddhist meditation techniques—single-minded concentration could be applied usefully in many situations.

In all walks of life we can benefit from focusing the mind and increasing memory.

SUMMARY FOR DAILY PRACTICE

1. Choose an object of meditation and focus your mind on it, trying to achieve and maintain stability, clarity, and intensity. Avoid laxity and excitement.

2. Alternatively, identify the fundamental state of the mind, unsullied by thought, in its own state—mere luminosity, the knowing nature of the mind. With mindfulness and introspection remain in that state. If a thought arises, just look into the very nature of that thought; this will cause it to lose its power and dissolve of its own accord.

IV

PRACTICING
WISDOM

8

Examining How Beings and Things Exist

❖

Overview of Wisdom in Spiritual Practice

To generate the type of love and compassion that motivates you to seek Buddhahood, not for yourself but for the sake of others, first you must confront suffering by identifying its types. This is the first noble truth. From the time we are born to the time we die we suffer mental and physical pain, the suffering of change, and pervasive suffering of uncontrolled conditioning. The second and third noble truths lead us to understand the causes of suffering and whether or not those causes can be removed. The fundamental cause of suffering is ignorance—the mistaken apprehension that living beings and objects inherently exist. This chapter will show that beings and objects, in fact, do not exist this way.

We all have a valid, proper sense of self, or "I," but then we additionally have a misconception of that "I" as inherently existing. Under the sway of this delusion, we view the self as existing under its own power, established by way of its own nature, able to set itself up. This sense of inherent existence can even be so strong that the self feels independent from mind and body. For instance, if you are weak from sickness, you might feel that you could switch bodies with someone who is stronger. Similarly, when your mind is dull, you might feel that you could switch your mind with someone else's sharp mind.

However, if there were such a separate I—self-established and existing in its own right—it should become clearer and clearer under the light of competent analysis as to whether it exists as either mind or body, or the collection of mind and body, or different from mind and body. In fact, the closer you look, the more it is not found. This turns out to be the case for everything, for all phenomena. The fact that you cannot find them means that those phenomena do not exist under their own power; they are not self-established.

Sometime during the early sixties when I was reflecting on a passage by Tsongkhapa about unfindability and the fact that phenomena are dependent on conceptuality, it was as if lightning coursed within my chest. Here is the passage:

A coiled rope's speckled color and coiling are similar to those of a snake, and when the rope is perceived in a dim area, the thought arises, "This is a snake." As for the rope, at that time when it is seen to be a snake, the collection and parts of the rope are not even in the slightest way a snake. Therefore, that snake is merely set up by conceptuality. In the same way, when the thought "I" arises in dependence upon mind and body, nothing within mind and body—neither the collection which is a continuum of earlier and later moments, nor the collection of the parts at one time, nor the separate parts, nor the continuum of any of the separate parts—is in even the slightest way the "I." Also there is not even the slightest something that is a different entity from mind and body that is apprehendable as the "I." Consequently, the "I" is *merely* set up by conceptuality in dependence upon mind and body; it is not established by way of its own entity.

The impact lasted for a while, and for the next few weeks whenever I saw people, they seemed like a magician's illusions in that they appeared to inherently exist but I knew that they actually did not. That experience, which was like lightning in my heart, was most likely at a level below completely valid and incontrovertible realization. This is when my understanding of the cessation of the afflictive emotions as a true possibility became real. Nowadays I always meditate on emptiness in the morning and bring that experience into the day's activities. Just thinking or saying "I" as in "I will do such and such" will often trigger the feeling. But still I cannot claim full understanding of emptiness.

A consciousness that conceives of inherent existence does not have a valid foundation. A wise consciousness, grounded in reality, understands that living beings and other phenomena—minds, bodies, buildings, and so forth—do not inherently exist. This is the wisdom of emptiness. Understanding reality exactly opposite to the misconception of inherent existence, wisdom gradually overcomes ignorance.

Remove the ignorance that misconceives phenomena to inherently exist and you prevent the generation of afflictive emotions like lust and hatred. Thus, in turn, suffering can also be removed. In addition, the wisdom of emptiness must be accompanied by a motivation of deep concern for others (and by the compassionate deeds it inspires) before it can remove the obstructions to omniscience, which are the predispositions for the false appearance of phenomena—even to sense consciousness—as if they inherently exist. Therefore, full spiritual practice calls for cultivating *wisdom* in conjunction with *great compassion* and the *intention to become enlightened* in which others are valued more than yourself. Only then may your consciousness be transformed into the omniscience of a Buddha.

SELFLESSNESS

Both Buddhists and non-Buddhists practice meditation to achieve pleasure and get rid of pain, and in both Buddhist and non-Buddhist systems the self is a central object of scrutiny. Certain non-Buddhists who accept rebirth accept the transitory nature of mind and body, but they believe in a self that is permanent, changeless, and unitary. Although Buddhist schools accept rebirth, they hold that there is no such solid self. For Buddhists, the main topic of the training in wisdom is emptiness, or selflessness, which means the absence of a permanent, unitary, and independent self or, more subtly, the absence of inherent existence either in living beings or in other phenomena.

Two Truths

To understand selflessness, you need to understand that everything that exists is contained in two groups called the two truths: conventional and ultimate. The phenomena that we see and observe around us can go from good to bad, or bad to good, depending on various causes and conditions. Many phenomena cannot be said to be inherently good or bad; they are better or worse, tall or short, beautiful or ugly, only by comparison, not by way of their own nature. Their value is relative. From this you can see that there is a discrepancy between the way things appear and how they actually are. For instance, something may—in terms of how it appears— look good, but, due to its inner nature being different, it can turn bad once it is affected by conditions. Food that looks so good in a restaurant may not sit so well in your stomach. This is a clear sign of a discrepancy between appearance and reality.

These phenomena themselves are called conventional truths; they are known by consciousness that goes no further than appearances. But the same objects have an inner mode of being, called an ultimate truth, that allows for the changes brought about by conditions. A wise consciousness, not satisfied with mere appearances, analyzes to find whether objects inherently exist as they seem to do but discovers their absence of inherent existence; it finds an emptiness of inherent existence beyond appearances.

Empty of What?

Emptiness, or selflessness, can only be understood if we first identify that of which phenomena are empty. Without understanding what is negated, you cannot understand its absence, emptiness. You might think that emptiness means nothingness, but it does not. Merely from reading it is difficult to identify and understand the object of negation, what Buddhist texts speak of as true establishment or inherent existence. But over a period of time, when you add your own investigations to the reading, the faultiness of our usual way of seeing things will become clearer and clearer.

Buddha said many times that because all phenomena are dependently arisen, they are relative—their existence depends on other causes and conditions and depends on their own parts. A wooden table, for instance, does not exist independently; rather, it depends on a great many causes such as a tree, the carpenter who makes it, and so forth; it also depends upon its own parts. If a wooden table or any phenomenon really were not dependent—if it were established in its own right—then when you analyze it, its existence in its own right should become more obvious, but it does not. This Buddhist reasoning is supported by science. Physicists today keep discovering finer and finer components of matter, yet they still cannot understand its ultimate nature. Understanding emptiness is even deeper.

The more you look into how an ignorant consciousness conceives phenomena to exist, the more you find that phenomena do not exist that way. However, the more you look into what a wise consciousness understands, the more you gain affirmation in the absence of inherent existence. Lust and hatred are ruled by ignorance, and so cannot be generated limitlessly.

Do Objects Exist?

Since, as we have established, when any phenomenon is sought through analysis, it cannot be found, you may be wondering whether these phenomena exist at all. However, we know from direct experience that people and things cause pleasure and pain, and that they can help and harm. Therefore, phenomena certainly do exist; the question is *how.* They do not exist in their own right, but only have an existence dependent upon many factors, including a consciousness that conceptualizes them.

Once they exist but do not exist on their own, they necessarily exist in dependence upon conceptualization. However, when phenomena appear to us, they do not at all appear as if they exist this way. Rather, they seem to be established in their own right, from the object's side, without depending upon a conceptualizing consciousness.

When training to develop wisdom, you are seeking through analysis to find the inherent existence of whatever object you are considering—yourself, another person, your body, your mind, or anything else. You are analyzing not the mere appearance but the inherent nature of the object. Thus it is not that you come to understand that the object does not exist; rather, you find that its inherent existence is unfounded. Analysis does not contradict the mere existence of the object. Phenomena do indeed exist, but not in the way we think they do.

What is left after analysis is a dependently existent phenomenon. When, for example, you examine your own body, its inherent existence is negated, but what is left is a body dependent on four limbs, a trunk, and a head.

If Phenomena Are Empty, Can They Function?

Whenever we think about objects, do we mistakenly believe that they exist in their own right? No. We can conceive of phenomena in three different ways. Let us consider a tree; there is no denying that it *appears* to inherently exist, but:

1. We could conceive of the tree as existing inherently, in its own right.
2. We could conceive of the tree as lacking inherent existence.

3. We could conceive of the tree without thinking that it inherently exists or not.

Only the first of those is wrong. The other two modes of *apprehension* are right, even if the mode of *appearance* is mistaken in the second and the third, in that the tree appears as if inherently existent.

If objects do not inherently exist, does this mean that they cannot function? Jumping to the conclusion that because the true nature of objects is emptiness, they are therefore incapable of performing functions such as causing pleasure or pain, or helping or harming, is the worst sort of misunderstanding, a nihilistic view. As the Indian scholar-yogi Nagarjuna says in his *Precious Garland,* a nihilist will certainly have a bad transmigration upon rebirth, whereas a person who believes, albeit wrongly, in inherent existence goes on to a good transmigration.

Allow me to explain. You need a belief in the consequences of actions to choose virtue in your life and discard nonvirtue. For the time being, the subtle view of the emptiness of inherent existence might be too difficult for you to understand without falling into the trap of nihilism, where you are unable to understand that phenomena arise in dependence on causes and conditions (dependent-arising). For the sake of your spiritual progress it would be better for now to set aside trying to penetrate emptiness. Even if you mistakenly believe that phenomena inherently exist, you can still develop an understanding of dependent-arising and apply it in practice. This is why even Buddha, on occasion, taught that living beings and other phenomena inherently exist. Such teachings are the thought of Buddha's *scriptures,* but they are not *his own* final thought. For specific purposes, he sometimes spoke in nonfinal ways.

In What Way Is Consciousness Mistaken?

Because all phenomena appear to exist in their own right, all of our ordinary perceptions are mistaken. Only when emptiness is directly realized during completely focused meditation is there no false appearance. At that time, the dualism of subject and object has vanished, as has the appearance of multiplicity; only emptiness appears. After you rise from that meditation, once again living beings and objects falsely appear to exist in and of themselves, but through the power of having realized emptiness, you will recognize the discrepancy between appearance and reality. Through meditation you have identified both the false mode of appearance and the false mode of apprehension.

❖

Let us return to the central point: All of us have a sense of "I" but we need to realize that it is only designated in dependence upon mind and body. The selflessness that Buddhists speak of refers to the absence of a self that is permanent, partless, and independent, or, more subtly, it can refer to the absence of inherent existence of any phenomenon. However, Buddhists do value the existence of a self that changes from moment to moment, designated in dependence upon the continuum of mind and body. All of us validly have this sense of "I." When Buddhists speak of the doctrine of selflessness, we are not referring to the nonexistence of this self. With this "I," all of us rightfully want happiness and do not want suffering. It is when we exaggerate our sense of ourselves and other phenomena to mean something inherently existent that we get drawn into many, many problems.

❖

SUMMARY FOR DAILY PRACTICE

As an exercise in identifying how objects and beings falsely appear, try the following:

1. Observe how an item such as a watch appears in a store when you first notice it, then how its appearance changes and becomes even more concrete as you become more interested in it, and finally how it appears after you have bought it and consider it yours.

2. Reflect on how you yourself appear to your mind as if inherently existent. Then reflect on how others and their bodies appear to your mind.

9

The Middle Way

❖

The Need for Both Concentration and Wisdom

Buddhist texts tell us that upon realizing emptiness, the illusion of inherent existence weakens, but this is unlikely after a single, brief realization. If you have not attained one-pointed concentration (calm abiding of the mind), you cannot use mere understanding of emptiness to uproot the illusion of inherent existence. Rather, you need to engage in analysis again and again; through concentrated meditation, your mind will become strong, deep, stable, and capable of one-pointed concentration on emptiness—which gradually works to diminish grosser levels of the misperception of reality.

This is the reason why Buddha's Sutras as well as the three lower Tantras all say that calm abiding (concentrated meditation) is a prerequisite for special insight (wisdom). The stabilizing meditation used in calm abiding and the analytical meditation used in special insight are not differentiated by the objects of meditation; both could have either emptiness or conventional phenomena as their focus. The difference is that observing emptiness from a state of calm abiding requires physical and mental suppleness induced through stabilizing meditation on emptiness, whereas special insight observing emptiness additionally involves physical and mental suppleness induced by analytical meditation with respect to emptiness. That degree of suppleness can only be gained after attaining the easier level of suppleness produced by stabilizing meditation. Therefore, you need to achieve calm abiding before special insight.

Although calm abiding could be achieved through taking emptiness as its object, this is only for practitioners who have already understood emptiness. Usually, however, practitioners first achieve one-pointed meditation and then gain the view of emptiness through reasoned analysis.

THE NEED FOR REASONING

All Buddhist schools agree that the analytical reasoning process which leads to an inference (a conceptual realization) derives from basic, shared, direct perception. As an example let us consider the following reasoning:

A plant does not inherently exist because of being a dependent-arising.

You begin by reflecting on the fact that a plant is a dependent-arising because its production depends on certain causes and conditions (such as a seed, soil, sunlight, and water), but eventually the reasoning process must be supported by direct perception, or it cannot stand. We can see with our eyes that plants change; they grow, mature, and finally dry up. In this sense, inference is blind, since it must eventually rely on direct perception. Inference depends on reasoning, which in turn rests on basic, shared, indisputable experience through direct perception.

Knowable objects can be divided into the obvious, the slightly obscure, and the very obscure. In order to understand a very obscure topic it is necessary to rely on scripture, but even for this type of inference it is not sufficient just to cite one scripture as validation for another. You must analyze whether:

- there are any internal contradictions among scriptures on that topic
- there is any contradiction between what the scripture says about that topic and what is evident in direct perception
- there is any contradiction between what the scripture says about that topic and what can be understood through basic inference, derived by reasoning.

So even in these very obscure cases based on scripture, analysis is needed.

Buddha set out four steps for establishing reliability:

1. Do not rely on just the person but rely on the doctrine.
2. With respect to the doctrine, do not rely on just the words but rely on the meaning.
3. With respect to the meaning, do not rely on just meaning requiring interpretation but rely on meaning that is definitive.

4. With respect to the definitive meaning, do not rely on just dualistic understanding but rely on the wisdom of direct perception of the truth.

Buddha also said:

> Like gold, upon being scorched, cut, and
>   rubbed,
> My word is to be adopted by monastics
>   and scholars
> Upon analyzing it well,
> Not out of respect [for me].

In the process of reasoning, it is very effective to state absurd consequences of wrong views in order to overcome the potency of that wrong idea, and then make a proof statement. When I was studying logic as a youth, a scholar once told me that, both in debate (with a Buddhist who asserts inherent existence) and in your own analytical meditation, it is a rather soft approach to use a syllogistic statement such as "My body is without inherent existence because it is a dependent-arising." However, it has more impact to use an absurd consequence such as "It follows that my body could not be a dependent-arising because it inherently exists," because it is fundamental to Buddhism that all phenomena are dependent-arisings.

COMPATIBILITY OF DEPENDENT-ARISING AND EMPTINESS

Buddha himself, in setting forth Sutras, and Nagarjuna and his spiritual sons—Aryadeva, Buddhapalita, and Chandrakirti—in commenting on the meaning of those Sutras, use the fact that phenomena are dependent-arisings as the *final* reason for establishing emptiness. This indicates that phenomena in general are not non-existent and that impermanent phenomena are fit to perform functions.

When Buddha taught the four noble truths, first he identified true sufferings, sources, cessations and paths, and then said:

> Sufferings are to be recognized, but there is nothing to be recognized. The sources of suffering are to be abandoned, but there is nothing to be abandoned. Cessation is to be actualized,

but there is nothing to be actualized. The path is to be meditated, but there is nothing to be meditated.

The meaning of this is that although there are factors among the four noble truths to be *conventionally* (and validly) recognized, abandoned, actualized, and meditated, there is nothing to be *ultimately* recognized, abandoned, actualized, and meditated. From the viewpoint of ultimate reality, all of these are beyond activity; everything has the same taste in the emptiness of inherent existence. In this way, Buddha set out the perspectives of the two truths—conventional and ultimate.

All phenomena—causes and effects, actions and agents, good and bad, and so forth—merely conventionally exist, only nominally exist; they are dependent-arisings. Because phenomena depend upon other factors for their existence, they are not independent. This absence of independence—or emptiness of inherent existence—is their own ultimate truth. You will come to comprehend this true emptiness of inherent existence when you become dissatisfied with mere appearances and you use analysis to probe beneath the surface.

When you thoroughly understand appearance and

emptiness, you will also understand that they are in harmony with one another. Appearance does not preclude emptiness, and emptiness does not preclude appearance. Failing to understand this you might believe in virtue, nonvirtue, cause and effect, and so forth, but then be unable to believe in emptiness. Similarly, you might think that you understand emptiness but then be unable to believe in the facts of cause and effect—help or harm, pleasure or pain—that arise dependent upon conditions. Without proper understanding, emptiness and appearance seem to prohibit each other.

However, phenomena are empty of inherent existence *because* they depend for their existence on other conditions. And conversely, phenomena are capable of functioning *because* they are empty of the solidity of inherent existence. If phenomena were not empty of inherent existence, if they *did* exist by their own power, then they could not be affected by other causes and conditions—they would not change. In that case, they would not cause pleasure and pain, help and harm. Good and bad would be impossible.

Full realization of dependent-arising brings with it the double understanding of appearance and emptiness of inherent existence. The extremes of utter nonexistence and inherent existence are simultaneously cleared away by this twin understanding. Knowing that phenomena arise prevents believing in the extreme of nihilism by allowing objects and beings to function in this world—allowing for the cause and effect of karma. Knowing that phenomena are dependent also prevents believing in the extreme of inherent existence by eliminating that phenomena exist in their own right. Through understanding these two truths, you arrive at the middle way.

The Heart Sutra

What is the relationship between objects and their emptiness? This profound topic is addressed in a scripture on the perfection of wisdom, called the *Heart Sutra,* which is recited and meditated daily throughout Great Vehicle Buddhist countries, such as China, Japan, Korea, Mongolia, Tibet, and Vietnam. It is a short and pithy presentation by Buddha about the wisdom required to overcome problems at their roots and—in conjunction with an other-directed motivation and compassionate deeds—to attain the omniscience of a Buddha. Here is the *Heart Sutra* in its entirety:

Homage to the supramundane victorious perfection of wisdom.

This is what I have heard: At one time, the Supramundane Victor was residing together with a great community of monastics and a great community of Bodhisattvas on Vulture Mountain in Rajagriha. At that time, the Supramundane Victor was absorbed in the concentrated meditation of the enumerations of phenomena called "perception of the profound." At that time the Bodhisattva great being, the Superior Avalokiteshvara, also was observing the practice of the profound perfection of wisdom and was viewing even these five aggregates [forms, feelings, discriminations, compositional factors, and consciousnesses] as empty of inherent existence.

Then, through the Buddha's power, the venerable Shariputra said to the Bodhisattva great being, the Superior Avalokiteshvara:

How should a child of good lineage—who wishes to practice the profound perfection of wisdom—train?

The Bodhisattva great being, the Superior Avalokiteshvara, replied to Shariputra:

Shariputra, sons or daughters of good lineage who wish to practice the profound perfection of wisdom should view [phenomena] as follows. They should correctly and thoroughly view even these five aggregates as empty of inherent existence. Form is emptiness; emptiness is form. Emptiness is not other than form; form is not other than emptiness. Similarly, feelings, discriminations, compositional factors, and consciousnesses are empty.

Shariputra, in that way all phenomena are empty—without characteristics, not produced, not ceasing, not defiled, not separated from defilements, not decreasing, not increasing. Therefore, Shariputra, in emptiness there are no forms, no feeling, no discriminations, no compositional factors, no consciousness, no eyes, no ears, no nose, no tongue, no body, no mind, no forms, no sounds, no odors, no tastes, no tangible objects, no [other] phenomena. In emptiness there is no eye constituent through to no mental constituent and through to no mental conscious-

ness constituent. In emptiness there is no ignorance and no extinguishment of ignorance
through to no extinguishment of aging and death.
Similarly, in emptiness there are no sufferings,
sources, cessations, and paths; no exalted wisdom,
no attainment, and also no nonattainment.

Therefore, Shariputra, since Bodhisattvas,
the great beings, have no attainment, they rely
on and reside in this profound perfection of
wisdom. Their minds are without obstruction
and without fear; having thoroughly passed
beyond error, they go to the finality of nirvana.
Even all the Buddhas in the past, present, and
future become manifestly and completely
awakened into unsurpassed, complete, perfect
enlightenment in reliance on this profound
perfection of wisdom.

Therefore, the mantra of the perfection of
wisdom is the mantra of great knowledge, the
unsurpassed mantra, the mantra equal to the
unequalled, the mantra thoroughly pacifying all
suffering. It should be known that since it is
not false, it is true. To state the mantra of the
perfection of wisdom:

Tadyata gate gate paragate parasamgate bodhi svaha. (It is thus: Proceed, proceed, proceed beyond, thoroughly proceed beyond, be founded in enlightenment.)

In that way, Shariputra, Bodhisattva great beings should train in the profound perfection of wisdom.

Then, the Supramundane Victor rose from that concentrated meditation and said to the Bodhisattva great being, the Superior Avalokiteshvara:

Good, good, good. Child of good lineage, it is so. It is so. In just the way that you have indicated, the profound perfection of wisdom should be practiced. Even the Ones Gone Thus admire this.

The Supramundane Victor having pronounced this, the venerable Shariputra, the Bodhisattva great being Avalokiteshvara, all those in the surrounding retinue, and the worldly beings—including gods, humans, demigods, and aroma-eaters—admired this and praised what the Supramundane Victor said.

Form and Emptiness

Drawing from a long tradition of Indian and Tibetan commentaries on the *Heart Sutra* I will offer some food for thought on its central passage: "Form is emptiness; emptiness is form. Form is not other than emptiness; emptiness is not other than form." This pithy statement contains much meaning:

1. All persons and things are dependent upon their causes and upon their parts and cannot exist independently of them. They are dependent-arisings; consequently they are empty of inherent existence. Because all phenomena are dependent-arisings, they have a nature of emptiness.

2. Conversely, as beings and things have no independent or inherent nature, they must rely on other factors. They must be dependent-arisings.

3. The emptiness of forms is not separate from forms. Forms themselves, which are produced and disintegrate due to the presence of conditions, are by their own nature empty of inherent existence.

4. This absence of inherent existence is their final reality, their mode of abiding, their final mode of being.

5. In sum, the production and disintegration, increase and decrease, and so forth of forms are possible because forms are empty of self-powered existence. Phenomena such as forms are said to dawn from within the sphere of the nature of emptiness.

Consequently, the *Heart Sutra* says, "Form is emptiness; emptiness is form; form is not other than emptiness; emptiness is not other than form." In this way, emptiness and dependent-arising are shown to be in harmony.

In brief, forms are not empty because of emptiness, forms themselves are empty. Emptiness means not that a phenomenon is empty of being some other object but that it itself is empty of its own inherent existence. That a form is emptiness means that the final nature of a form is its natural lack of inherent existence; because forms are dependent-arisings, they are empty of an independent self-powered entity. That emptiness is form means that this natural lack of inherent existence—which is the absence of a self-powered principle—makes possible the forms which are its sport or which are established from it in dependence upon conditions. Since forms are the bases of emptiness, emptiness is form; forms appear as like reflections of emptiness.

In my own experience it is easier to understand that because things are dependent-arisings they are empty of inherent existence than it is to understand that because things are empty, they must be dependent-arisings. Although intellectually I know the latter very well, experience on the level of feeling is more difficult. Nowadays I often reflect on a statement in Nagarjuna's *Precious Garland*:

> A person is not earth, not water,
> Not fire, not wind, not space,
> Not consciousness, and not all of them.
> What person is there other than these?

First he considers whether the physical elements of the body—earth (hard things), water (fluids), fire (heat), wind (air), and space (the empty spaces such as the gullet)—could be the self. Next he examines consciousness. Then he considers whether the collection of all of these could be the self. Finally, he rhetorically asks whether the self could be other than these. In none of these ways can the self be found.

Then Nagarjuna does not immediately draw the conclusion that the self is not real. Rather, right after that stanza, he says that the self is not nonexistent but is a dependent-arising which is set up dependent upon those six constituents named above. Then, based on this fact of dependence, he draws the conclusion that the self is not real:

> Due to being [set up in dependence upon] a
>   composite of six constituents,
> A person is not real.

Here, "not real" does not *just* mean that the self cannot be found when sought from among or separate from the six constituents. Nagarjuna is making the point that although the mind realizing the emptiness of inherent existence sees a mere absence, that very mind promotes an understanding that the self is a dependent-arising. I feel that the way he presents this is full of impact, avoiding both the extreme of holding that the self inherently exists and the extreme of holding that the self does not exist at all.

Like the two sides of the hand, when looked at one way by examining its deeper nature, there is the emptiness of inherent existence, but when looked at from the other side, there is the appearance of the phenomenon itself. They are one entity. Therefore, form is emptiness, and emptiness is form.

You have to be able to understand that the import of emptiness is also the meaning of dependent-arising. They are deeply connected. As your insight into emptiness grows clearer, you will see more and more that objects depend on causes and conditions and on their parts, and they bring about pleasure and pain *because* they do not exist inherently. If you come to feel that everything is useless because it is empty, you are mistaking emptiness for nihilism. Properly understanding emptiness means realizing how we must rely on cause and effect. The natural and full understanding of emptiness means a profound understanding of the union of appearance and emptiness.

❖

The understanding of emptiness is fantastic, is it not? It can serve as an antidote to the misconception of inherent existence, and yet in itself it also assists in greater understanding of cause and effect. That is real understanding of emptiness. It is impossible to explain the import of the realization of emptiness in the context of just hearing or reading an explanation. It is something that has to be worked at over a long period of time together with the practices of morality—refraining from harm and extending compassion—and through making supplications to Buddhas, Bodhisattvas, and other teachers for help in overcoming obstacles. We need many positive causes.

SUMMARY FOR DAILY PRACTICE

Frequently reflect on how phenomena arise in dependence on causes and conditions, and try to see how this opposes the way persons and things appear to be so solidly existent, to exist in their own right, to exist inherently. If you tend toward nihilism, reflect more on dependent-arising. If, by concentrating on causes and conditions, you tend to reinforce the inherent existence of phenomena, then put more emphasis on how dependence contradicts this so-solid appearance. You will probably be pulled from one side to the other; the true middle way takes time to find.

IO

Mind and the Deep
Nature of Mind

❖

In a scripture on perfect wisdom, Buddha makes the
following profound statement:

> In the mind, the mind is not to be found; the
> nature of the mind is clear light.

To understand the levels of meaning in this statement, you have to identify what the mind is, analyze its
deeper nature, and investigate how good and bad effects
come about. Let us examine the various parts of the
statement.

1. The phrase "in the mind" is concerned with what mind is—its luminous and knowing nature. In Chapter Seven, on concentrated meditation, we talked about the luminous and knowing nature of the mind and how, although it exists throughout every moment of mind, it is necessary to set aside previous thoughts and not begin new ones in order to identify it.

2. When Buddha says "the mind is not to be found," this indicates that luminosity and knowing nature are not the mind's deepest and final nature. Rather, the ultimate nature of the mind is "clear light," its emptiness of inherent existence.

You might think Buddha is saying that the mind does not exist, but this is not the case. I, as the explainer, am explaining this statement through the workings of my own mind, and you, the reader, are reading by the workings of your mind. We are always using the mind, and it is always right with us, but we do not know it well. Thus, even though it is difficult to identify the mind, it exists and is being analyzed as to whether it is its own deep nature.

It is clear that the mind exists, but since it is not established as its own final nature and basic disposition, what is its mode of being? Its deep nature is a mere emptiness of its own inherent existence. This means that the faulty defilements that pollute the mind—such as ignorance, lust, and hatred—are temporary, and therefore separable from the mind. Once these defilements are understood to be superficial and not in the mind's basic nature, we see that the deep nature of the mind is clear light, emptiness.

DEFILEMENTS ARE SUPERFICIAL, THE NATURE OF THE MIND IS CLEAR LIGHT

Buddhist texts explain in different ways the statement, "Defilements are superficial, the nature of the mind is clear light." Still, this is not a matter of Buddha's saying something so vague that it could be interpreted in any way one wishes. Rather, it has many different explicit and implicit meanings. In Highest Yoga Tantra there are many ways of drawing meaning out of an abstruse statement. One can explain its literal meaning, its general meaning, its hidden meaning, and its final meaning.

To clarify Buddha's statement, "Defilements are superficial, the nature of the mind is clear light," in combination with Tantra, I will cite the *Magical Array Tantra* which is a section in the *Repetition of the Names of Manjushri Tantra*:

> The perfect Buddhas arise from A.
> A is the supreme of letters.

From among the four meanings listed above, I will give a *general* explanation of this statement. The letter A is a negative particle in Sanskrit. It indicates emptiness, which is the absence, or negation, of inherent existence. When the *Magical Array Tantra* says that "The perfect Buddhas arise from A," this means that the Buddhas dawn from within the noumenal sphere of emptiness; or, put another way, the Buddhas dawn from meditating on the emptiness of inherent existence. Through meditation, defilements are extinguished in the noumenal sphere of reality (the emptiness of inherent existence). Emptiness, symbolized by A, is the supreme topic, and therefore the *Magical Array Tantra* says, "A is the supreme of letters."

Also, from the viewpoint of Highest Yoga Tantra, the letter A refers to the indestructible drop within which a Buddha body is achieved. In Highest Yoga

Tantra, Buddhahood arises by concentratedly focusing on the indestructible drop at the heart center. The final body of a Buddha has the nature of the indestructible drop. This adds to our understanding of the statement that the perfect Buddhas arise from the letter *A*.

What is the indestructible drop? It is the union of the very subtle wind and the very subtle mind. Mind knows objects, whereas wind, or inner energy, causes consciousness to engage objects. Since this is the case, with a union of wind and mind there are changes in consciousness.

BEGINNINGLESS MIND

Consciousness is nonphysical. It does not have a color or shape or the obstructive quality of physical things. Its entity is mere luminosity and cognition, and when it meets with certain conditions (such as when an object is present and a sense faculty is functioning properly), it reflects that object. That the mind changes from moment to moment, and appears in different aspects, indicates that the mind operates under the other-influence of causes and conditions.

A mind arises in dependence upon a former mind of similar type, which requires that there has been an earlier beginningless continuum of mind. If the production of a mind did not need to depend upon former moments of mind but could just be produced causelessly, then a mind could be produced anywhere and any time, which is absurd. Similarly, if consciousness was not produced as a continuation of a former entity of consciousness and instead were produced from something physical, either it would always, absurdly, be produced or it would never be produced, which is also absurd. This indicates that consciousness is a continuation of a former entity of consciousness.

Because consciousness is based in a former moment of consciousness, there can be no beginning to its continuum. There is no beginning of consciousness, and there is no end to it. This continuum makes possible the transformation of the mind into improved states. When the mental continuum is associated with impure states, our experience is limited to the realm of cyclic existence. When the mental continuum breaks free from impure states, we can achieve nirvana. In this way, all phenomena are the artifice, or sport, of the mind. The impure phenomena of cyclic existence are the sport of impure mind; the pure phenomena of nirvana are the sport of pure mind.

FAULTY STATES OF MIND DEPEND
UPON IGNORANCE

Since it is said that "In the mind, the mind is not to be found; the nature of the mind is clear light," impure states of mind such as desire and hatred are not part of the nature of mind and must be produced by ignorance—a consciousness misconceiving inherent existence—either in the present moment or from an earlier source. All faulty states of mind have mistaken consciousness as their root. Ignorance is a form of consciousness that is mistaken with respect to the object of its attention; it is wrong about it; it has no valid cognition as its root.

A mistaken awareness and an awareness with a valid foundation have contradictory ways of apprehending phenomena, so the one harms the other. When, in your practice, you become accustomed to correct attitudes, faulty states of mind naturally diminish until finally they are extinguished.

The very system of the Buddhist teaching is based on natural contradiction. We want happiness and do not want suffering. The pain we seek to avoid mainly stems from mental attitudes, and since the source of mental suffering is afflictive emotions either directly or indirectly, we have to consider whether there are any forces opposing them. If, for instance, anger causes suffering, then we must find a contradictory force. For anger it is love and compassion. Although anger and love/compassion are all consciousnesses, they have contradictory ways of apprehending the same object. Their realizations are opposites. Similarly, if a room is too hot, there is no way to reduce the heat but to introduce cold. Just as heat and cold oppose each other, so too do opposing mental states, pure and impure. To the extent you develop one, the other decreases. Therefore, it is possible to remove faulty states of mind. Antidotes exist.

UNION OF THE CONVENTIONAL AND THE ULTIMATE

The mind itself is a conventional truth; the reality of the mind, its emptiness of inherent existence, is its ultimate truth. These two truths are contained in one indivisible entity. Just as there is a union of the two truths, conventional and ultimate, with respect to the mind, so there is a union of the two truths with respect to each and every object: Its appearance is a conventional truth; and its emptiness of inherent existence is its ultimate truth.

Final reality is known through the reasoning of dependent-arising. For instance, because the mind is a dependently arisen entity, the mind is empty of inherent existence. When you understand emptiness through the reasoning of dependent-arising, you realize that all phenomena are unions of dependent-arising and emptiness; appearance and emptiness are perceived as harmonious.

Dependently arisen appearances of conventional phenomena provide the context for teaching compassion—called "the vast path," as there is such a huge variety of appearances. The emptiness of the inherent existence of appearances provides the basis for teaching what is known as "the profound path," because emptiness is the *final nature* of phenomena—peaceful, free from conceptualizations, and of one taste. Through meditatively cultivating these two paths—the vast aspect of compassion and the profound wisdom of emptiness—in an inseparable way, faulty states of mind in your continuum undergo gradual transformation. They are gradually removed, and the excellent attributes of a Buddha's mind and body emerge.

Buddhahood is achieved through the unified cultivation of both motivation and wisdom. However, motivation and wisdom have their own respective imprints on Buddhahood. The result of cultivating motivation is the Form Bodies of a Buddha, which exist for the sake of fulfilling the well-being of others. The imprint of cultivating wisdom is the Truth Body of a Buddha, which is the fulfillment of your own development. What are the main forms of motivation and wisdom? The primary motivation is an other-directed intention to become enlightened, inspired by love and compassion and inspiring the practice of compassionate deeds such as giving, morality, and patience. The main form of wisdom is an intelligent consciousness realizing the emptiness of inherent existence.

The foundations of Buddhism have three aspects. The *basis* is the two truths, conventional and ultimate. From these two truths the *path* emerges with the twin factors of motivation and wisdom, each related to its respective truth. The *fruit,* or result of travel on the path, is actualization of the two bodies—the Form Bodies and Truth

Body of a Buddha. To bring this all together, on the *basis* of the two truths—conventional and ultimate—you practice the two qualities of the *path*—motivation and wisdom—which leads you to achieve the *fruit,* the Form and Truth Bodies of a Buddha.

SUMMARY FOR DAILY PRACTICE

1. Identify the luminous and knowing nature of the mind, unclouded by thoughts.
2. Probe the deeper nature of the mind again and again to reveal its absence of inherent existence, its emptiness, by reflecting on the mind's dependence on causes and conditions and dependence on parts—including the fact that any length of time that passes in the mind depends on earlier and later parts of that time period.
3. Try to realize the compatibility of the appearance of the mind with its emptiness of inherent existence; see how these two mutually support each other.

V
TANTRA

11

Deity Yoga

❖

In Buddhism there are basically two types of practices: Sutra and Tantra. So far we have been discussing Sutra practice. The special purpose of Tantra is to provide a faster path so that qualified practitioners can be of service to others more quickly. In Tantra the power of imagination is harnessed to meditation in a practice called deity yoga. In this practice you imagine 1) replacing your mind as it ordinarily appears, full of troubling emotions, with a mind of pure wisdom motivated by compassion; 2) substituting your body as it ordinarily appears (composed of flesh, blood, and bone) with a body fashioned from compassionately motivated wisdom; 3) developing a sense of a pure self that depends on purely appearing mind and body in an ideal environment, fully engaged in helping others. As this distinctive practice of Tantra calls for visualizing yourself with a Buddha's body, activities, resources, and surroundings, it is called "taking imagination as the spiritual path."

Let us consider a qualm about this practice. You are considering yourself to have Buddha qualities which you presently do not have. Is this, then, a correct type of meditative consciousness? Yes. Your mind is involved in understanding reality, out of which you are appearing as a deity. Therefore, your mind, from this viewpoint, is correct. Also, you are *purposely* imagining yourself as having a divine body even if you do not presently possess one. This is an imaginative meditation; you are not convinced from the depths that you actually have pure mind, body, and selfhood. Rather, based in clear imagination of ideal body and mind, you are cultivating the sense of being a deity, compassionately helping others.

To be a *special* trainee of Tantra—that is to say, the kind of trainee for whom Buddha specifically set forth the practice of Tantra—a practitioner must have sharp faculties and have already attained stable wisdom realizing emptiness, or be ready for speedy activation of this wisdom. The requirements for just practicing Tantra are less rigorous; still, to engage in Tantra at any level demands a powerful intention to become enlightened for the sake of others, and a feeling that this needs to be done very quickly.

At the beginning of Tantric practice, the basic way to develop calm abiding is to meditate on your own body as if it were that of a deity. When you meditate on a divine body, first you meditate on emptiness, gaining as much awareness of the emptiness of inherent existence as you can. When you have acclimated to this state, you use that very mind itself as the basis out of which the deity appears. The mind, realizing emptiness, appears as the deity and his or her surroundings. First you meditate on emptiness; out of that the deity appears; then you concentrate on the deity.

In this way, deity yoga combines wisdom and compassionate motivation; a single consciousness realizes emptiness and also appears compassionately in the form of an altruistic deity. In the Sutra system, although there is a union of wisdom and compassionate motivation, the practice of wisdom is only *affected* by the force of the practice of motivation, and the practice of motivation is only *affected* by the force of the practice of wisdom; they are not contained within one consciousness. A distinguishing feature of Tantra is that they are. Inclusion of motivation and wisdom within one consciousness is what makes Tantra's progress so swift.

When I was a young boy, Tantra was just a matter of blind faith. At age twenty-four I lost my own country, and then after coming to India started really reading Tsongkhapa's explanations on emptiness. Then, after moving to Dharamsala, I put more effort into the study and practice of the stages of the path, emptiness, and Tantra. So it was only in my late twenties after gaining some experience of emptiness that deity yoga made sense.

One time in the main temple in Dharamsala I was performing the ritual of imagining myself as a deity of Highest Yoga Tantra, called Guhyasamaja. My mind continuously remained on the recitation of the ritual text, and when the words "I myself" came, I completely forgot about my usual self in relation to my combination of mind and body. Instead, I had a very clear sense of "I" in relation to the new, pure combination of mind and body of Guhyasamaja that I was imagining. Since this is the type of self-identification that is at the heart of Tantric yoga, the experience confirmed for me that with enough time I could definitely achieve the extraordinary, deep states mentioned in the scriptures.

INITIATION

To practice Tantra it is especially important to gain access to the transmission of blessings from previous great beings. Blessings also exist in Sutra practice, but they are crucial in Tantra. The first means of entry to these blessings is through the door of initiation. There are four classes of Tantras—Action, Performance, Yoga, and Highest Yoga Tantra—each with it own initiations to ripen the mind for practice, and each with its own meditations.

Where do you receive initiation? In a mandala, comprised of ideal surroundings and divine residents which all are manifestations of compassion and wisdom. There are mandalas of varying complexity for all four Tantras. Some are painted. Others are constructed from colored sands, and still others comprise a special class of concentration mandalas.

In order to receive initiation and to take vows in a mandala of Yoga Tantra or Highest Yoga Tantra, the lama conducting the ceremony must have the full complement of qualifications. All four sets of Tantras place special emphasis on the attributes of the lama, in keeping with Buddha's detailed descriptions of teachers' qualifications for the various stages of the path. Remember also Buddha's admonition to rely not just on the person but on the doctrine. You should not be overwhelmed by a teacher's reputation. Most important, the teacher must know the doctrine, the practices, well.

Pledges and Vows

In the two lower Tantra sets—Action and Performance—there is no clear indication that Tantric vows must be taken upon initiation; nevertheless, there are many pledges to be kept. In the two higher Tantra sets—Yoga and Highest Yoga—after receiving initiation with all of its facets, you must take Tantric vows in addition to pledges. Yoga Tantra and Highest Yoga Tantra have fourteen basic vows as well as lists of infractions to guard against, but as they differ in their respective paths, even the basic vows differ slightly. Since the practice of Tantra is mainly concerned with overcoming the *appearance* of yourself and your surroundings as ordinary (in order to overcome the *conception* of these as ordinary), you visualize yourself to have a Buddha's body, compassionate activities, resources, and abode. Therefore, most of the pledges are concerned with substituting ideal for ordinary appearances, and restraining your own estimation of yourself, your companions, your environment, and your activities as being ordinary.

Except for the particular vow of individual liberation that lasts for just twenty-four hours, all of the other vows of individual liberation are taken for an entire lifetime (although it is possible to rescind one's vows and give back one's ordination). By contrast, Bodhisattva and Tantric vows extend right through to the time of highest enlightenment, as long as one has not committed a root infraction.

First one assumes the morality of individual liberation, then Bodhisattva morality, and finally Tantric morality. Householders who take the Bodhisattva and Tantric vows keep a householder's version of the vows of individual liberation. The *Kalachakra Tantra,* which flourished during the eleventh century in India and became a principal Tantra of the New Translation Schools in Tibet, states that if there are three teachers of Tantra, one with householder's vows, another with the vows of a novice monastic, and a third with the vows of a full-fledged monastic, the person who has taken the vows of a full-fledged monastic should be considered higher than the others. This indicates the high estimation that even this Tantric system places on the monastic morality. The *Guhyasamaja Tantra* says that externally you should keep the discipline of the practice of individual liberation, and internally maintain an affinity for the practice of Tantra. In these ways the practice of Sutra and Tantra work together.

USING SEX IN THE PATH

Let us begin to consider the role of sexual desire in the path in Tantra by looking at the prohibition against sexual misconduct in the morality of individual liberation, which is entirely based on the principle of refraining from harm. Specific sexual misconduct is identified in detail in Vasubandhu's *Treasury of Manifest Knowledge.* For a male it would be to cohabit with someone else's wife, or with someone who is under the care of her family. For a female it is the same; it is prohibited to cohabit with someone else's husband or with someone who is under the care of his family. Some have suggested, ridiculously, that since Vasubandhu's text explains the ten nonvirtues from the viewpoint of a male, there is no fault if a female engages in the non-virtues—and thus there are no prohibitions for a female!

For Buddhists, sexual intercourse can be used in the spiritual path because it causes a strong focusing of consciousness if the practitioner has firm compassion and wisdom. Its purpose is to manifest and prolong the deeper levels of mind (described earlier with respect to the process of dying), in order to put their power to use in strengthening the realization of emptiness. Otherwise, mere intercourse has nothing to do with spiritual cultivation. When a person has achieved a high level of practice in motivation and wisdom, then even the joining of the two sex organs, or so-called intercourse, does not detract from the maintenance of that person's pure behavior. Yogis who have achieved a high level of the path and are fully qualified can engage in sexual activity, and a monastic with this ability can maintain all the precepts.

One Tibetan yogi-adept, when criticized by another, said that he ate meat and drank beer as offerings to the mandala deity. Such Tantric practitioners visualize themselves as deities in a complete mandala, within realization that the ultimate deity is the ultimate bliss—the union of bliss and emptiness. He also said that his sexual practice with a consort was undertaken for the sake of developing real knowledge. And that indeed is the purpose. Such a practitioner can make spiritual use not only of delicious meat and drink, but even of human excrement and urine. A yogi's meditation transforms these into real ambrosia. For people like us, however, this is beyond our reach. As long as you cannot transform piss and shit, these other things should not be done!

Buddha set out a specific series of stages on the path precisely for this reason. The preliminary stage is training in the vows of individual liberation. If you live as a monk or nun, your conduct has a more sound basis—there is little danger of excessive distraction. Even if you cannot fully implement such vows, there is not much risk. Then simply practice, practice, practice. Once you develop inner strength, you can control the four internal elements—earth, water, fire, and wind (or five elements if inner space is included). Once you can fully control these internal elements, then you can control the outer five elements. Then you can make use of anything.

How does sexual intercourse help in the path? There are many different levels of consciousness. The potential of grosser levels is very limited, but the deeper, more subtle levels are much more powerful. We need to access these subtler levels of mind. But in order to do so, we need to weaken and temporarily stop grosser consciousness. To accomplish this it is necessary to bring about dramatic changes in the flow of inner energies. Even though brief versions of the deeper levels of mind occur during sneezing and yawning, they obviously cannot be prolonged. Also, previous experience with manifesting the deeper levels is required to make use of their occurrence in deep sleep. This is where sex comes in. Through special techniques of concentration during sex, competent practitioners can prolong very deep, subtle, and powerful states and put them to use to realize emptiness. However, if you engage in sexual intercourse within an ordinary mental context, there is no benefit.

A Buddha has no use for sexual intercourse. Deities depicted in a mandala are often in union with a consort, but this does not suggest that Buddhas have to rely on sexual intercourse for their bliss. Buddhas have full bliss within themselves. Deities in union spontaneously appear in mandalas for the benefit of people with very sharp faculties who can make use of a consort and the bliss of sexual union in practicing the quick path of Tantra. In much the same way, the Tantric Buddha Vajradhara appears in peaceful aspects and wrathful aspects, but this does not mean that Vajradhara has these two aspects to his personality. Vajradhara is always totally compassionate. Rather, his spontaneous appearance in various ways is for the sake of trainees. Vajradhara appears in just the way that the trainee should meditate when using afflictive emotions such as lust or hatred in the process of the path. To corral such powerful emotions into the spiritual path trainees cannot be imagining that they have the peaceful body of Shakyamuni Buddha. Deity yoga is required. Since in the case of hatred, for instance, it is necessary to meditate on your own body in a fierce form, Vajradhara automatically appears in the appropriate ferocious form to show the trainee how to meditate. The same is true for sexual yoga; trainees who are capable of using the bliss arising from the desire involved in gazing, smiling, holding hands, or union must perform the appropriate deity yoga; they could not be imagining themselves as Shakyamuni, a monk.

The purpose of Vajradhara's various appearances is neither to scare the trainees nor to excite desire in them, but to show how to do imaginative meditation in those forms in order eventually to overcome afflictive emotions.

A Buddha is capable of appearing spontaneously without exertion in whatever way is appropriate. The form of these appearances is shaped by the needs of others, not for the sake of that Buddha. From a Buddha's own point of view, that Buddha has the total self-fulfillment of the Truth Body, in which he or she remains forever.

Remember that Tantric morality is built on the morality of individual liberation and on the morality of compassion. The aim of Tantra is to achieve Buddhahood on a faster path in order to be of service to others more quickly.

❖

SUMMARY FOR DAILY PRACTICE

Since the practice of Tantra is primarily to transform
how you see yourself, others, the environment, and your
activities, it can be helpful to visualize yourself as having
a compassionate motivation, a pure body, and conduct
that benefits others.

VI

STEPS ALONG
THE WAY

12

Overview of the Path to Enlightenment

❖

GRADUAL PROGRESS

How does a practitioner gradually proceed to Buddhahood through meditatively cultivating the paths of motivation and wisdom? In the *Heart Sutra,* Buddha expresses the levels of the path in a short, profound statement, *"Tadyata gate gate paragate parasamgate bodhi svaha,"* (pronounced "Tadyata gatay gatay paragatay parasamgatay bodee svaha") which means: "It is thus. Proceed, proceed, proceed beyond, thoroughly proceed beyond, be founded in enlightenment." Let us examine this more closely, starting with the first word, *"gate"* ("proceed" or "go"). Who is proceeding? It is the "I" or self that is designated in dependence upon the continuum of the mind. From what are you proceeding? You are moving away from cyclic existence, that state of being under the influence of contaminated actions and counterproductive emotions. To what are you proceeding? You are proceeding to Buddhahood endowed with a Truth Body, forever free of suffering and the sources of suffering (afflictive emotions), as well as the predispositions established by afflictive emotions. Upon what causes and conditions do you depend as you proceed? You are proceeding in dependence on a path that is a union of compassion and wisdom.

Buddha is telling trainees to go to the other shore. From the viewpoint of the trainee, cyclic existence is on the near side, it is close at hand. On the far shore, a distant place, is nirvana—the state of having passed beyond suffering.

THE FIVE PATHS

When Buddha says, *"Tadyata gate gate paragate parasamgate bodhi svaha"* ("It is thus: Proceed, proceed, proceed beyond, thoroughly proceed beyond, be founded in enlightenment"), he is telling trainees to proceed over the five paths:

> *gate*—the path of accumulation;
> *gate*—the path of preparation;
> *paragate*—the path of seeing;
> *parasamgate*—the path of meditation;
> *bodhi*—the path of no more learning.

Let us identify the nature of spiritual advancement over these five paths:

1. What is the initial path, the *path of accumulation?* It is that period when you mainly practice other-directed motivation and thereby accumulate great stores of merit. Also, although you are practicing a union of motivation and wisdom, your realization of emptiness has not reached the level of mutually supportive stabilizing meditation and analytical meditation called "a state arisen from meditation." On this path you achieve powerfully concentrated meditation, and are working toward a state arisen from meditation realizing emptiness.

2. At the point at which you achieve a state of wisdom

arisen from meditation realizing emptiness, you pass to the *path of preparation.* By becoming more and more familiar with this state, together with cultivating compassionate motivation, you gradually perceive the appearance of emptiness more clearly over the four levels of the path of preparation (heat, peak, forbearance, and highest mundane qualities).

3. Eventually emptiness is realized directly, without even subtle contamination from dualistic appearance, which has vanished. This is the beginning of the *path of seeing*—the path of initial direct realization of the truth concerning the deep nature of phenomena. At this point in the Great Vehicle, the ten Bodhisattva levels (called grounds because on them special spiritual qualities are engendered) begin. During the path of seeing and path of meditation, two types of obstructions, intellectually acquired and innate, are respectively overcome. Intellectually acquired states of mind come about through adherence to false systems. For example, there are followers of some Buddhist schools who believe that phenomena conventionally exist by way of their own character, based on the unfounded

"reasoning" that if phenomena were not established in this way, they could not function. This kind of misconception, polluted by an invalid system of tenets, is called artificial, or intellectually acquired. Even if you have acquired no new predispositions through wrong conceptual thinking in this lifetime, everyone has in their mental continuum predispositions established by adhering to wrong views in former lifetimes.

By contrast, innate faulty states of mind have existed in all sentient beings—from insects to humans—since beginningless time, and operate of their own accord without depending on faulty scripture and reasoning.

4. Intellectually acquired, or artificial, obstructions are removed through the path of seeing, whereas innate obstructions are more difficult to overcome (because you have been conditioned to these faulty states of mind since beginningless time). They must be removed by continued meditation on the meaning of emptiness. Because such meditation must take place repeatedly over a long period of time, this phase of the path is called the *path of meditation*. Indeed, you have meditated on emptiness

earlier, but the path of meditation refers to a path of extended familiarization.

On this level you pass through the remaining nine Bodhisattva grounds. From among the ten grounds, the first seven are called impure, the last three are called pure. This is because on the first seven grounds you are still in process of removing afflictive obstructions and thus these seven are not yet purified. Through the first part of the eighth ground you are removing afflictive emotions. The balance of the eighth, ninth, and tenth grounds enable you to overcome the obstructions to omniscience.

5. Now, through using the diamondlike concentrated meditation achieved at the end of the ten Bodhisattva grounds—the culmination of still having obstructions yet to be overcome—you can effectively undermine the very subtle obstacles to omniscience. The very next moment of your mind becomes an omniscient consciousness, and simultaneously the deep nature of the mind becomes the Nature Body of a Buddha. This is the fifth and final path, the *path of no more learning*. From the very subtle wind, or energy—which is one entity with that

mind—various pure and impure physical forms spontaneously spring forth to assist sentient beings; these are called the Form Bodies of a Buddha. This is Buddhahood, a state of being a source of help and happiness for all sentient beings.

Let me take a moment here to address the many misconceptions about whether or not women can attain Buddhahood. In the Sutra Great Vehicle, there is no indication that a woman cannot achieve Buddhahood. However, the texts state that, during the practices for accumulating merit over three periods of countless great eons, you will arrive at a time when the karma you are working at will mature as the physical marks and beauties of a Buddha; at this time, according to the Sutra Great Vehicle, it helps to have strong physical support, so you naturally come to have the body of a male. Those texts also say that in the final lifetime before you achieve Buddhahood, you need to have the body of a male. However, Highest Yoga Tantra, which we consider to be the final system, says that not only can a woman achieve Buddhahood but she can do so right in this lifetime.

QUALITIES OF BUDDHAHOOD

In all forms of Buddhism, practice is based on the intention to leave cyclic existence. Additionally, in the Great Vehicle you are motivated by the other-concerned intention to become enlightened. In Tantra, through techniques that enhance the development of the concentrated meditation which is the union of calm abiding and special insight, you can achieve the state of Buddhahood in which all obstructions—the afflictive obstructions preventing liberation from cyclic existence and the obstructions to omniscience preventing Buddhahood—have been removed.

A Buddha's qualities are described as different "bodies" which can be divided into two general types:

◆ the Truth Body, for the fulfillment of your own welfare
◆ the Form Bodies, for the fulfillment of others' welfare.

Form Bodies, in turn, can be divided by how they appear to beings on different levels of purity and impurity: Highly advanced trainees can access the Complete

Enjoyment Body. Other levels of trainees experience a wide variety of Emanation Bodies. The Truth Body can also be divided into two types, the Nature Body and the Exalted Wisdom Body. The Nature Body can be further subdivided into a state of natural purification and a state of purification of adventitious (or caused) defilements. The Exalted Wisdom Truth Body can be further divided according to many different viewpoints. Maitreya's *Ornament for Clear Realization* specifies twenty-one sets of uncontaminated exalted wisdoms which can be subdivided into one hundred and forty-six sets.

PRACTICING FOR THE LONG HAUL

This has been a brief explanation of: the ground—the two truths, conventional and ultimate; the paths built on that ground—motivation and wisdom; the fruits of the paths—the Form Bodies and Truth Body of a Buddha. It is helpful to have this overview of the structure of practice, but you need to remember that realization is generated through many causes and conditions—proper understanding, accumulation of merit, and overcoming of obstructions. If you have not first accumulated merit and purified ill deeds, it is difficult to gain realization just from trying to meditate. Therefore it is important to work through each of the prerequisites.

Engagement in the prerequisites is not just a matter of filling some sort of count, or even of completing retreat for three years and three phases of the moon (as some might imagine from the fact that many retreats take this long), or for any other period of time. Instead, you must accumulate merit and purify obstructions until certain realizations are generated. You may spend your entire lifetime doing so, with the goal of improving future lives. Sometimes, because of a lack of knowledge, people who perform long retreats end up with considerable pride about the mere fact that they finished the retreat. The increase in pride yields an increase in anger, jealousy, and competitiveness. The same can happen with mere book knowledge of doctrine. It is not easy; afflictive emotions are tricky.

Practice is not something you do for a couple of weeks or a couple of years. It takes place over many lifetimes, for eons and eons. As we have seen, some texts say enlightenment is achieved after accumulating the collections of merit and wisdom for three periods of countless great eons. If you consider this statement properly, it can encourage you to adopt a patient, persistent attitude through difficult circumstances. If learning this saddens you, this could be due to your desire to achieve Buddhahood swiftly out of your great concern for others. It could also be a sign of insufficient courage. Enlightenment cannot be attained without working hard at it. To believe otherwise means you are harboring some form of selfishness.

❖

This is the entire process of the path. Even though Tibetans might not have wealth that can be kept in a wallet, they have this wealth that is kept in the mind! The stated good intentions of the various religions are not sufficient; we must implement them in daily life in society. Then we can know the real value of their teachings. If a Buddhist, for instance, meditates in a temple but outside the temple does not enact those contemplative ideals, that is not good. We must practice in daily life.

The real value of practice is seen when we face a difficult period. When we are happy and everything goes smoothly, then practice seems not so urgent, but when we face unavoidable problems such as sickness, old age, death, or other desperate situations, it becomes crucial to control your anger, to control your emotional feelings, and to use your good human mind to determine how to face that problem with patience and calm.

If we practice this way, our first hope is that we may overcome the problem, but, if not, at least the problem cannot disturb your mental peace. That is good, is it not? You are facing the situation and retaining your peace of mind—without taking drugs or trying to pull your thoughts away from it. That is why we take such great interest in our weekends and vacations! Five days a week you are very busy, working hard to make money, then on the weekend you go to some remote place with that money and have a nice time! This means you are trying to take your mind off your problem. But the problem is still there.

However, if you have a good mental attitude, it is not necessary to divert yourself. When you can face the situation and analyze the problem, then, like a big piece of ice in the water, it will gradually melt away. If you practice sincerely, you will experience its real value.

According to Buddha's own word, his teaching will

last here for five thousand years. At the end of that five thousand years it will finally be destroyed by someone who is a reincarnation of Buddha himself, since when that day comes there will be no further value in the teaching. However, there are a billion world systems like ours, with limitless billions of those. In some of them the teaching is newly being introduced; in some it is waning. The teaching continually remains somewhere at all times. The Buddhas never disappear, and the teaching never vanishes.

❖

SUMMARIES FOR DAILY PRACTICE

Here in one place are the summaries for practice gathered from throughout the book. Focus on ones suitable for your level at this point. Or, you could alternate among them over the course of a week. Cultivated patiently over time, the practices will become more and more familiar, and your life will become more meaningful.

Morality of Individual Liberation

1. Examine your motivation as often as you can. Even before getting out of bed in the morning, establish a nonviolent, nonabusive outlook for your day. At night examine what you did during the day.

2. Notice how much suffering there is in your own life:

   ◆ There is physical and mental pain which you naturally seek to avoid, such as sickness, aging, and death.

   ◆ There are temporary experiences, like eating good food, that seem to be pleasurable in and of themselves but, if partaken continuously, turn into pain—this is the suffering of change. When a situation switches from pleasure to pain, reflect on the fact that the deeper nature of the original pleasure is revealing itself. Attachment to such superficial pleasures will only bring more pain.

   ◆ Reflect on how you are caught in a general process of conditioning that, rather than being under your control, is under the influence of karma and afflictive emotions.

3. Gradually develop a realistic view of the body through examining its constituents—skin, blood, flesh, bone, and so forth.

4. Analyze your life closely. You will eventually find it difficult to misuse it by becoming machinelike or by merely seeking money as a surrogate for happiness.

5. Adopt a positive attitude in the face of difficulty. Imagine that by undergoing a difficult situation you are also undermining worse consequences from other karmas that you would otherwise have to experience in the future. As a mental exercise, take upon yourself the burden of everyone's suffering of that type.

6. Evaluate the possible negative and positive effects of feelings such as lust, anger, jealousy, and hatred. When it becomes obvious that their effects are harmful, you will have arrived at the conclusion that there are no positive results of, say, anger. Analyze more and more, and gradually your conviction will strengthen; repeated reflection on the disadvantages of anger will cause you to realize that it is senseless, and even pathetic. This decision will cause your anger gradually to diminish.

7. Having recognized the scope of suffering, research its

cause, and identify that the source of suffering is ignorance of the true nature of persons and things, and that
lust, hatred, and so forth are based on this ignorance.
Realize that suffering can be removed, can be extinguished into the sphere of reality. Reflect that this true
cessation is attained through the practice of morality,
concentrated meditation, and wisdom—true paths.

8. Notice your attachments to food, clothes, and
shelter, and adapt monastic practices of contentment
to a layperson's life. Be satisfied with adequate food,
clothing, and shelter. Use the additional free time for
meditation so that you can overcome more problems.

9. Develop a strong wish to refrain from harming others,
either physically or verbally, no matter whether you are
embarrassed, insulted, reviled, pushed, or hit.

Morality of Concern for Others

Perform the five-step visualization for developing compassion:

1. Remain calm and reasonable.
2. In front of you to the right, imagine another version of yourself, egotistical and self-centered.

3. In front of you to the left, imagine a group of poor people, suffering beings who are unrelated to you, neither friend nor enemy.

4. Observe these two sides from your calm vantage point. Now think, "Both want happiness. Both want to get rid of suffering. Both have the right to accomplish these goals."

5. Consider this: Just as usually we are willing to make temporary sacrifices for a greater long-term good, so the benefit of the larger number of suffering beings to your left is much more important than this single egotistical person on your right. Notice your mind naturally turning to the side of the greater number of people.

Perform the ritual for the aspiration to enlightenment. First take the seven preliminary steps:

1. *Make homage* to Shakyamuni Buddha surrounded by innumerable Bodhisattvas, whom you imagine filling the sky in front of you.

2. *Offer* all wonderful things—whether you own them or not—including your body, your resources, and your own virtue, to the Buddhas and Bodhisattvas.

3. *Disclose* the countless ill deeds of body, speech, and mind you have perpetrated with an intent to harm others. Regret having done them, and intend to abstain from them in the future.

4. *Admire* from the depths of the heart your own virtues and those of others. Take joy in the good things you have done in this and previous lives, thinking, "I really did something good." Take joy in the virtues of others, including those of Buddhas and Bodhisattvas.

5. *Entreat* the Buddhas who have become completely enlightened but have not yet taught, to teach for the sake of those who suffer.

6. *Supplicate* the Buddhas not to pass away.

7. *Dedicate* these six practices to attaining highest enlightenment.

Then undertake the central part of the ritual for aspiring to enlightenment:

1. With a strong determination to attain Buddhahood in order to serve other beings, imagine a Buddha in front of you, or your spiritual teacher as a representative of Buddha.

2. Recite three times as if you are repeating after him or her:

> Until I reach enlightenment I seek refuge in Buddha, the doctrine, and the supreme spiritual community.
>
> Through the collections of merit of my giving, morality, patience, effort, concentration, and wisdom, may I achieve Buddhahood in order to help all beings.

To maintain and strengthen this profound altruism in this life perform the following:

1. Recall again and again the benefits of developing an intention to become enlightened for the sake of others.
2. Divide the day into three periods and the night into three periods, and during each of those periods take a little time out or rouse yourself from sleep and practice the five-step visualization given earlier. It is also sufficient to visualize the five steps three times in one morning session that lasts around fifteen minutes, and three times in one night session for fifteen minutes.

3. Avoid mentally neglecting the welfare of even one being.
4. As much as possible, engage in virtuous activity with a good attitude, and develop a rough understanding of the nature of reality, or maintain a wish to do so and work at it.

To maintain and strengthen this profound altruism in future lives:

1. Do not lie to anyone at all, unless you can help others greatly through lying.
2. Directly or indirectly help people to progress toward enlightenment.
3. Treat all beings with respect.
4. Never cheat anyone, and always remain honest.

In essence, think again and again, "May I become able to help all beings."

Concentrated Meditation

1. Choose an object of meditation and focus your mind on it, trying to achieve and maintain sta-

bility, clarity, and intensity. Avoid laxity and excitement.

2. Alternatively, identify the fundamental state of the mind unsullied by thought, just in its own state—mere luminosity, the knowing nature of the mind. With mindfulness and introspection remain in that state. If a thought arises, just look into the very nature of that thought itself; this will cause it to lose its power and dissolve of its own accord.

Wisdom

As an exercise in identifying how objects and beings falsely appear in perception, try the following:

1. Observe how an item such as a watch appears in a store when you first notice it, then how its appearance changes and becomes even more concrete as your interest grows, and finally how it appears after you have bought it and consider it yours.

2. Notice at various times how you yourself appear to your mind as if existent in and of yourself, without depending on mind and body.

3. Then, frequently reflect on how phenomena arise in dependence on causes and conditions, and observe how this contradicts the way people and things appear to exist in their own right, to exist inherently. If you tend toward nihilism, reflect more on dependent-arising. If, by concentrating on causes and conditions, you tend to reinforce the inherent existence of phenomena, put more emphasis on how dependence contradicts this so-solid appearance. You will probably be pulled from one side to the other; the true middle way takes time to find.

Also:

1. Identify the luminous and knowing nature of the mind, unclouded by thoughts and without any conceptual overlay.
2. Probe the deeper nature of the mind repeatedly to reveal its absence of inherent existence, its emptiness. Reflect on the mind's dependence on causes, conditions, and parts. For the mind, any length of time of the mind—whether one minute or the shortest moment—depends on earlier and later parts of that time period.

3. Try to realize the compatibility of the appearance of the mind with its emptiness of inherent existence; see how these two mutually support each other.

Tantra

Since the practice of Tantra is primarily to transform how you see yourself, others, and the environment, it can be helpful to visualize yourself as having a compassionate motivation, pure body, and activities benefiting others.

Though my own knowledge is limited and my experience is also very poor, I have tried my best to help you understand the full breadth of the Buddha's teaching. Please implement whatever in these pages appears to be helpful. If you follow another religion, please adopt whatever might assist you. If you do not think it would be helpful, just leave it alone.

Selected Readings

H.H. the Dalai Lama, Tenzin Gyatso. *The Dalai Lama at Harvard.* Translated and edited by Jeffrey Hopkins; coedited by Elizabeth Napper. Ithaca, N.Y.: Snow Lion Publications, 1989.

————*Kindness, Clarity, and Insight.* Translated and edited by Jeffrey Hopkins; coedited by Elizabeth Napper. Ithaca, N.Y.: Snow Lion Publications, 1984.

————*The Meaning of Life.* Translated and edited by Jeffrey Hopkins. Boston: Wisdom Publications, 2000.

Hopkins, Jeffrey. *Buddhist Advice for Living and Liberation: Nagarjuna's Precious Garland.* Ithaca, N.Y.: Snow Lion Publications, 1998.

———*Cultivating Compassion.* New York: Broadway Books, 2001.

Lopez, Donald S. *The Heart Sutra Explained.* Albany, N.Y.: State University of New York Press, 1988.

Wallace, Vesna A., and B. Alan Wallace. *A Guide to the Bodhisattva Way of Life.* Ithaca, N.Y.: Snow Lion Publications, 1997.